SNOW FA

NOTES

including
- *Life and Background of the Author*
- *Introduction to the Novel*
- *Historical Introduction to the Novel*
- *A Brief Synopsis*
- *List of Characters*
- *Critical Commentaries*
- *Critical Essays*
- *Review Questions and Essay Topics*
- *Selected Bibliography*

by
Richard Wasowski, M.A.

WILEY
Wiley Publishing, Inc.

Editor	Copy Editor
Greg Tubach	Tina Sims
Project Editor	Production
Tammy S. Castleman	Wiley Indianapolis Composition Services

CliffsNotes™ *Snow Falling on Cedars*

Published by:
Wiley Publishing, Inc.
909 Third Avenue
New York, NY 10022
www.wiley.com

CONTENTS

Center Spread: The Characters

SNOW FALLING ON CEDARS

Notes

LIFE AND BACKGROUND OF THE AUTHOR

Although he received critical praise for his collection of short stories and his nonfiction treatise on the value of home schooling, David Guterson's third book and first novel, *Snow Falling on Cedars*, was purchased by Harcourt Brace for only $15,000, after several other publishers rejected it. *Snow Falling on Cedars* went on to win the PEN/Faulkner award, among others, and provided Guterson with popular as well as critical success.

Childhood and Undergraduate Education. Guterson was born the third of five children on May 4, 1956, to Murray and Shirley Guterson, in Seattle, Washington. His father was a criminal lawyer and somewhat of a local celebrity. Guterson credits his father for teaching him two important tenets for life: "Find something you love to do—before you think about money—and do something that you feel has a positive impact on the world." Guterson spent his childhood outdoors, with fishing being one of his most popular pastimes. During his teenage years he committed what he called "minor acts of rebellion and delinquency," and led, overall, what he called an average existence.

When he enrolled in the University of Washington, Guterson first studied a variety of assorted courses, including anthropology and oceanography, but during his junior year, he enrolled in a short-story writing course, and "from day one I felt like this was it." Guterson had found his calling in life—to be a writer.

Guterson earned his B.A. in 1978, and married Robin Ann Radwick, January 1, 1979. They moved to Rhode Island when he enrolled in the graduate writing program at Brown University, but Guterson didn't care for it, claiming it was "too experimental." He attended only a semester, and soon after, the couple returned to the Northwest.

Graduate School and Family Life. Guterson returned to the University of Washington and studied with Charles Johnson, who would later win the National Book Award for *Middle Passage*. Johnson served as a mentor to Guterson, introducing him to the ideas of John Gardner. Gardner shared with Guterson his vision of the moral responsibility of writers. Guterson considers himself "a traditional storyteller" in the Gardner tradition.

In 1982, Guterson earned his Master of Fine Arts (M.F.A.) and began submitting stories for publication; he received many rejection slips. Eventually, literary magazines and journals accepted some of his stories. Six of the accepted stories, plus four new ones, became *The Country Ahead of Us, the Country Behind* (1989). This collection deals with such diverse themes as alienation, the failure to take on the responsibilities of love, and emotional sustenance. Though a well-reviewed fiction collection, the book didn't sell many copies. Years later, looking back on his early stories, Guterson referred to them as "flawed but interesting."

The strength of the collection's publication led to pieces being submitted to *Sports Illustrated* and *Esquire*; working as a freelance journalist, Guterson eventually impressed *Harper's* so much that he became a contributing editor for the magazine. Guterson tended to submit long and detailed pieces of nonfiction. One piece became his first nonfiction book, *Family Matters: Why Home Schooling Makes Sense* (1992). This expansion of his *Harper's* article about home schooling championed the way that Guterson and his wife were educating their own four children, Taylor, Henry, Travis, and Angelica.

Snow Falling on Cedars. Though his children were home-schooled, Guterson taught high school English for ten years. Often his students read *Romeo and Juliet* and *To Kill a Mockingbird*; both works share similar themes with *Snow Falling on Cedars*, Guterson's first novel. Guterson also admits to copying the structure of *To Kill a Mockingbird*, where two separate stories become one, in his fiction debut. The description "a courtroom drama with racial conflict . . . as well as being a regional novel that portrays a particular time in U.S. history" could pertain to either *Mockingbird* or *Cedars*.

When asked about his writing, Guterson stated, "My work is rooted in the Northwest. It's all I know." The people and places of the Northwest dominate the pages of *Snow Falling on Cedars*, published in 1994. Stylistically, *Snow Falling on Cedars* is considered literary fiction, and critics praised Guterson's attention to detail. Winning the PEN/Faulkner Award (the largest annual juried prize for fiction in the United States) and receiving word-of-mouth recommendations led to an incredible paperback sales success.

This newfound success was nice, but Guterson's goal wasn't to publish popular fiction. "I'm not interested in writing merely to entertain. I want to explore philosophical concerns." One of these concerns is how our individual decisions affect not only our lives but also the lives of those with whom we come in contact. He views the universe as a troubling place and told the *Washington Post,* "for me—and this is why I wrote the book—it's about the fact that we human beings are required by the very nature of our existence to conduct ourselves carefully. It's about the fact that in an indifferent universe . . . the only thing we can control is our own behavior."

Careful not to preach, though, and wanting readers to reflect on a set of ideals, Guterson believes that "fiction writers shouldn't dictate to people what their morality should be," and "not enough writers are presenting moral questions for reflection." For Guterson, asking questions differs greatly and distinctively from giving answers.

Post–*Snow Falling* Activity. After the success of his first novel, Guterson continued to write essays for magazines as he researched and wrote his next book. Hollywood embraced his text, and a big-screen movie version of *Snow Falling on Cedars* was released in the winter of 1999. Guterson's second novel, *East of the Mountains*, released in April of 1999, also features a protagonist who survived World War II. Fans of *Snow Falling on Cedars* were not disappointed.

INTRODUCTION TO THE NOVEL

On the surface, *Snow Falling on Cedars* is about the murder trial of Kabuo Miyamoto, an American of Japanese descent charged with murdering Carl Heine, a fellow salmon fisherman; however, the trial really provides a framework for an analysis of the effect that the internment of Japanese-Americans during World War II had on the people of San Piedro Island, a small island in the Pacific Northwest. *Snow Falling on Cedars* opens in present-day 1954, at the start of Kabuo's trial, but the narrative moves back and forth in time. The trial itself takes only three days, but the novel spans the pre-war, World War II, and post-war eras. The novel explores the effects of war, the difficulties of race, and the mystery of human motivation. The characters act and react to one another and with one another in a combination murder mystery and courtroom drama, as well as provide the story of a doomed love affair. The text taken as a whole is a meditation on prejudice and justice and the effect that one has on the other.

On San Piedro, everyone is either a fisherman or a berry farmer, and because World War II scarred everyone, a decade later the islanders are still trying to establish some semblance of normalcy. This proves difficult, though, since the Japanese islanders—many of whom were American citizens—were taken away and imprisoned during the war. Upon their return, those of Japanese descent faced prejudice, grudges, and anti-Japanese sentiment, and those who were interned had some prejudices of their own. So did the land dispute or the wartime internment lead to the circumstances of Carl Heine's death? Only circumstantial evidence and a possible motive exist to accuse Kabuo, but nonetheless, he is jailed for 77 days and is tried in court.

Points of view shift during the telling of the story, as Guterson uses flashback not only to show how the characters perceive the events of the alleged murder but also to reveal what had happened before and during the war. Two main stories unfold and eventually merge. One of the reporters covering the trial is Ishmael Chambers, he himself a war veteran, but Ishmael is not an objective observer: Because of the war, he has lost his arm and the love of his life.

Guterson explores a variety of related themes, including how racism can and does undermine justice in a court of law. He also examines the notions of fairness and forgiveness on a personal and social level, along with the feeling of alienation. Connections exist between justice and morality; between love, betrayal, and redemption; and between a character's public and private trial. All these things are examined and re-examined as Kabuo's trial continues.

Guterson's novel was generally well received, with his knowledge of the Pacific Northwest and his attention to detail garnering him the most praise. Many critics consider *Snow Falling on Cedars* a great story but an even better rendering of people and place. His descriptions of the island and the people who live there have been called "incredible." His control of the dialogue and the novel's pacing have been deemed "impressive," and the development of all characters, including important but relatively minor ones, enables Guterson to "find big truths in mundane places."

Some question Guterson's style, however, claiming that *Snow Falling on Cedars* doesn't know whether it's a serious mystery or social commentary. These critics don't seem to like the way Guterson weaves fiction with social commentary, or else they think he just didn't succeed in what he attempted to do. Those complaints are in the minority of popular and critical opinion. Most readers tend to recognize that prejudice on either side of a relationship can lead to misunderstandings and that someone living with one foot in two different cultures is not fully a part of either.

Snow Falling on Cedars is an example of literary fiction that sold remarkably well; in fact, the paperback edition became the fastest selling novel in Vintage history. Winning the PEN/Faulkner and the Barnes and Noble Discovery (for new writers) awards, as well as having glowing verbal recommendations, didn't hurt sales either. Guterson can't explain the popularity of his text and isn't sure he understands it, but he sums up his experience with "A well-written book speaks for itself." Because *Snow Falling on Cedars* speaks for itself so eloquently, the book is well on its way to becoming one of American literature's new classics.

HISTORICAL INTRODUCTION TO THE NOVEL

Japanese cultural considerations inform Guterson's *Snow Falling on Cedars*. From the first century AD until the early nineteenth century, Japan was ruled under a feudal system that included a class known as the samurai. These powerful men directed personal armies of *doshin* and fought to maintain land ownership, regional influence, and societal order. The samurai prided themselves on honor, ancestry, bravery, and fighting skills. Their training began at a young age with mental discipline, a broad education that included poetry and reading, and instruction on social manners. In preparation for battle, the samurai trained in all aspects of war, including horse riding, knot tying, and sword fighting. The goal of the samurai was to achieve perfection on both the battlefield and in his personal life.

Samurai also believed in Buddhism and practiced the art of meditation—a state they were taught to enter by keeping their heads erect and their backs straight—as a way to calm their minds. Buddhists view desire and greed as the cause of all human suffering. They believe the end to suffering is by living a life on the Middle Path, between luxury and hardship. Truthful speech, actions done for goodness rather than reward, and a mindfulness of self are three important actions that Buddhism encourages. Buddhists admire and seek to have compassion, kindness, patience, and humility. Anything done in a deliberate way reflects back on the doer. If the motivation behind an action is dishonest, then the return will be negative. All people are part of a chain, and who they are today influences who they will become tomorrow.

Interestingly, farmers were just below samurai in the feudal system, with craftsmen, merchants, and religious all beneath them. Farmers were held in a higher regard because of their ability and responsibility to feed the nation. This centuries-old attitude of farming as a noble profession bears some influence on the willingness of Japanese immigrants to accept employment in farming situations that were undesirable to many Americans.

The Japanese internment during World War II serves as a backdrop to the novel. Prior to the attack on Pearl Harbor, anti-Asian prejudice was not a new situation in the United States, especially in the West. Chinese laborers working on the U.S. railroads and then Japanese laborers working on farms and fisheries were viewed as undesirable. Organizations like the Japanese Exclusion League and the Native Sons & Daughters of the Golden West sought to remove the Asians from the economy and the region. Japanese immigrants were prevented from owning land, but they worked hard and became successful in spite of societal limitations. By 1941, Japanese farmers produced 33 percent of the vegetables grown in California. The surprise bombing of Pearl Harbor brought World War II onto the doorstep of the United States. The 127,000 persons of Japanese descent living in the United States became enemies of the state, even though 67 percent of them were American citizens by birth. The U.S. government arrested and questioned prominent men of Japanese descent. Many Americans feared that the entire race was capable of spying for the Japanese government.

On February 19, 1942, President Franklin Roosevelt signed Executive Order 9066, which allowed the Secretary of War to designate and prescribe military areas "from which any or all persons may be excluded." Against the advice of the Attorney General and the Director of the FBI, the military declared western Washington, all of Oregon and California, and half of Arizona a military area within which any person of Japanese descent, regardless of citizenship, could not live. Persons of Italian and German heritage—in spite of the war in Europe—weren't included in the relocation effort, but Japanese-Americans were instructed to report to the assembly centers, taking only what they could carry. They were denied their 5th Amendment rights against deprivation of life, liberty, and prosperity and due process of the law.

Faced with sometimes as little as 48 hours to liquidate their possessions, they sold belongings for a small fraction of their worth. Businesses and homes built from hard work and sacrifice were lost as Japanese were moved by armed troops first to assembly centers and then to one of ten concentration centers in the deserts of California, Utah, and Arizona; remote regions of Colorado, Idaho, and Wyoming; and swampland in Arkansas. Lieutenant General John DeWitt and the War Relocation Authority (WRA) oversaw the transfer of the Japanese descendents into the camps. The wartime shortage of lumber and building materials meant that the hastily built camps were sparsely constructed. Several families were housed within barracks with plumbing limited to a centralized kitchen and latrine. Barbed wire and guard towers housing military personnel surrounded the camps. Travel outside the camps wasn't permitted until August of 1942, when the Department of Labor issued an urgent request for agricultural workers. With so many men serving military duty, the government was forced to use Japanese laborers to harvest crops in Colorado, Utah, Montana, and Idaho. The men were paid $12 to $19 a month for their work—with the understanding that they were only on an agricultural leave from the internment camp.

As the war continued, Nisei men (Americans of Japanese descent) were allowed to form the 100th Battalion and the 442nd Army Combat Regiment, which became the most decorated unit, with 9,486 Purple Hearts bestowed on them for military valor. Nisei students were also allowed out of the camps if they could find a university to accept them, provided the university wasn't in a declared military zone, wasn't near a railway, and didn't have an ROTC program. Finding programs that met these criteria proved to be very difficult. The camps remained open until December 17, 1944, when a public proclamation declared them closed just one day before the Supreme Court was expected to rule on the legality of the situation.

Upon their release, detainees were given $25 and train fare home. Many, however, had no home to return to. The Claims Act of 1948 allowed claims for property loss to be filed for compensation. Although claims of $148 million were filed, only $37 million was paid. Pride, physical and mental illness, or a desire to forget the incident have been among the reasons that more people didn't apply for financial reimbursement from the government.

On August 10, 1988, President Ronald Reagan signed a Civil Rights bill that gave $20,000 and an apology to each surviving detainee. The money and words are small compensation for the lives and opportunities taken from the Japanese immigrants and their children. Today, the Manzanar Camp in California serves as an historic landmark so that people won't forget the actions that occurred on America soil.

In addition to the Japanese internment during World War II, agriculture and fishing—two main occupational options that existed for men in the Pacific Northwest in the post-World War II era—also inform the novel. Both professions were more than just jobs; they were ways of life.

The landowners were the farmers, growing crops best suited to the environment. During the picking season, Japanese and Indian immigrants worked the fields. On San Piedro, strawberries were the cash crop.

If a man wasn't a farmer, then he was most likely a fisherman. During the 1950s, fishermen used gill nets extensively. These nets hung like curtains in the water and were so named because fish were trapped in the mesh by their gills. As the fishing industry

became more and more competitive and
gill nets were created—some miles long in
caught not only fish but also birds, turtle:
forms of wildlife. Outrage by various er.
groups led to regulations outlawing such exte.
ing; however, gill nets are used illegally to this

kept th
Ishma
Hatsu
her s
coul<
sepa

A BRIE

Jap
Ha
A
K

San Piedro, a small island in the Pacific Northw
salmon fishermen and strawberry farmers. It is also l
Japanese-Americans. *Snow Falling on Cedars* opens ii
Fielding's courtroom as the trial of one of thes<
Americans, Kabuo Miyamoto, who is on trial for killing l
erman Carl Heine, Jr., commences.

The story line of Kabuo's trial is the only one in *Snow l*
Cedars that is told in chronological order. Early testimony
sheriff and his deputy provides the facts in the case: The)
called to investigate the drifting of the *Susan Marie*, Carl's
and they found his body in his own fishing nets. Although the ;
iff announced that Carl's death was an accident, everything di<
quite add up, so he got a warrant to search Kabuo's boat, t.
Islander, for the murder weapon. Finding blood on the butt end <
Kabuo's fishing gaff, the sheriff arrested him.

As the trial progresses, the facts of Kabuo's case are revealed,
as is the truth about what happened that night. Throughout the
three-day trial, stories and history are told and retold from shifting
perspectives and points of view; information is leaked slowly and
deliberately, and two separate story lines develop in the form of
memory and testimony.

The first major story line is the interracial love story. Kabuo's
wife, Hatsue, shares a past with the island's only reporter, Ishmael
Chambers. Their connection is established in the first chapter, but
the extent of their involvement is revealed gradually. They grew up
together, playing on the beach, looking for crabs, and shared a first
kiss. Years later they kissed again, and a secret, teenage love affair
blossomed. They didn't tell their families or their friends. At school
they acted like strangers. Because of their cultural differences, they

ᴇir interracial relationship hidden. During their senior year, ł was certain he was falling more and more in love with ᵢ, while she was becoming more and more confused about nse of responsibility to herself and her family. Before they work through their feelings for one another, they were ated.

Jatsue and her family were sent to Manzanar, a World War II nese internment camp. There her mother found out about sue's affair and pressured her into writing a "Dear John" letter. Manzanar, Hatsue, determined to get on with her life, marries buo.

After receiving the letter from Hatsue, Ishmael hates her, and ᴇ harbors this hate for years. During the war, he loses his arm, nd his hate grows. After the war, he sees her around the island, vith her children, and he is still bitter. He views the trial as his ᴄhance to get back in her life, no matter what the cost.

Besides providing the background to the interracial love story, memories and testimony also provide the story of an illegal land deal that was never completed. Carl Heine, Sr., agreed to sell seven acres of land to Zenhichi Miyamoto, Kabuo's father, in an agreement that sidestepped existing laws. This lease-to-own agreement lasted eight years. During the war, Carl Sr. died, and because of his internment, Zenhichi Miyamoto missed the last two payments. Carl's wife, Etta, who never approved of her husband's deal anyway, sold the land to Ole Jurgensen.

Kabuo visited both Ole Jurgensen and Etta Heine after the war, staking claim to the seven acres he refers to as his family's land. He even offered to buy it back, but Jurgensen isn't interested. Ten years later, after a stroke rendered him unable to work all of his land, Jurgensen put his farm up for sale. Carl junior stopped by right after the sign went up and made a deal to buy the land; earnest money changed hands. Later that same day, Kabuo stopped by and was devastated to learn that he arrived too late. Kabuo then approached Carl junior, asking him to sell the seven acres of land to him. Carl agreed to think about it.

At this point, toward the end of Kabuo's trial, the two separate story lines merge. For the most part, the interracial love story was private, whereas the quarrel over the land was more public. Clearly, Kabuo had both a motive and a method to kill Carl.

Carl Heine, Sr.

Carl's father. He made the original agreement with Zenhichi Miyamoto (Kabuo's father) to sell the seven acres, but died before the affairs were settled. He, like Arthur Chambers, is one of the few islanders who don't categorize people by their skin color.

Etta Heine

Carl's mother. She is the most outspoken bigot in the story. She distrusts and dislikes all people of Japanese descent. She speaks her mind and is convinced she did nothing wrong when she didn't follow her husband's agreement, an agreement she never approved of and considered wrong. She is also convinced that Kabuo killed her son, and she will tell only the testimony that supports that assertion.

Susan Marie Heine

Carl's widow. Her memories provide telling testimony about Carl's character, though she didn't know everything about her husband.

Arthur Chambers

Ishmael's father. He started the *San Piedro Review* and tried to remain objective during the war. Not all islanders cared for his views. Ishmael continued the paper after Arthur's death.

Nels Gudmundsson

Kabuo's court-appointed attorney. He knew he needed to earn Kabuo's trust before he would learn the truth about happened on the night in question. An elderly, experienced litigator, he knows his way around the courtroom. He also knows that the court of popular opinion has already found Kabuo guilty.

Alvin Hooks

The prosecutor. His job is to present the case, with all the damning evidence. He is competent and quick, and when new testimony and assertions are added to the mix late in the day, he responds adroitly and effectively. His case is quite compelling, but is it 100 percent accurate?

Ole Jurgensen

Farmer who purchased land from Etta Heine. After the war, he sold the land back to Carl Jr. because a stroke left him unable to care for it.

Art Moran

The sheriff. He's in charge of investigating Carl's death. Initially, Art states that the death was accidental, but too many things don't quite add up, and eventually he charges Kabuo with murder. He is satisfied that the mooring rope and the gaff with Carl's blood are more than enough evidence to convict Kabuo.

Abel Martinson

The deputy. He assists Sheriff Moran as best he can, but investigation isn't his strong suit.

Llewellyn Fielding

The judge. Llewellyn controls the pace of the legal proceedings, directing what is admissible and inadmissible, and instructs the jurors in regards to their legal obligations, insisting for them to "stay objective, be reasonable." (Much—although not all—of the evidence against Kabuo is circumstantial.) Because Judge Fielding follows his own advice, he is competent and fair during the proceedings.

Horace Whaley

The Island County coroner. His wartime memories prevent him from being entirely objective when giving his testimony. Although he knows that the cause of Carl's death was drowning, he still implies that Carl was forced overboard by encouraging Sheriff Moran to "start looking for a Jap with a bloody gun butt."

Mrs. Shigemura

Hatsue's teacher. She taught many of the island girls of Japanese descent what it means to be a Japanese woman. Most of what Hatsue knew of her parents' culture came from her.

Erik Syvertsen

The fisherman who found the *Susan Marie* adrift.

Bjorn Andreason

Islander who purchased Etta Heine's home.

Ed Soames

The courtroom bailiff.

Mrs. Eleanor Dokes

The court stenographer.

William Gjovaag, Marty Johansson, Dale Middleton, and Leonard George

Island fishermen.

Mr. Niita

A berry farmer. When they were young, Hatsue, Ishmael, and Kabuo all picked berries for him.

CRITICAL COMMENTARIES

CHAPTERS 1–3

Guterson uses the first three chapters to provide the necessary exposition for the legal thriller, the interracial love story, the exploration of racism, and the social commentary. The three-day trial proceeds in a straightforward fashion, but the rest of the narrative is a combination of flashback and memories. Events are told through different points of view, with testimony seamlessly becoming memory, with people and words triggering other memories and feelings. When Ishmael Chambers is introduced, it's not readily apparent that he's the main character of *Snow Falling on Cedars*.

The narrative opens in a courtroom; Kabuo Miyamoto, an American of Japanese descent, is on trial for killing Carl Heine, Jr. The trial takes place on the small island of San Piedro, north of the Puget Sound in the Pacific Northwest. Alvin Hooks is prosecuting, and Nels Gudmundsson is defending Kabuo. Moments before the trial starts, the owner, editor, and reporter for the local newspaper, Ishmael Chambers, shares a stilted conversation—and obviously a past—with Kabuo's wife, Hatsue: "'Go away,' she'd said in a whisper, and then for a moment she'd glared. He remained uncertain afterward what her eyes had meant—punishment, sorrow, pain."

Sheriff Art Moran, the first witness for the prosecution, provides his account of the events that transpired. Art heard a radio report that Carl Heine's boat, the *Susan Marie*, was drifting in the bay. Art and his deputy, Abel Martinson, investigated and found the *Susan Marie* empty; the fishing nets were not. They lifted the nets aboard the boat and proceeded to examine Carl Heine's corpse. Nels Gudmundsson, Miyamoto's lawyer, conducts the cross-examination, emphasizing the fact that it was possible that the wound on Carl's head may have been inflicted after his death: "'is it possible, Sheriff Moran, that the deceased banged his head sometime *after* his death? Is that possible?'"

The action and development of the first three chapters provide the impression that *Snow Falling on Cedars* is solely going to be a courtroom drama; however, as the opening paragraphs depict Kabuo Miyamoto sitting in the courtroom while snow falls on the cedars surrounding the small island courthouse, Guterson introduces the important weather motif and symbolism. Snow falls throughout the trial, covering, freezing, beautifying, and cleansing, while at the same time isolating the inhabitants of the island.

Guterson mentions all the important themes, characters, and information used in the multiple narratives, yet he draws no attention to the most important information. His eye for detail is precise, providing a clear sense of time and place—the setting—which plays a pivotal part in one of the novel's major themes. The history between Ishmael and Hatsue is mentioned at the very end of

Chapter 1, but instead of using this as a transition into their story and their history, Chapter 2 opens with the first witness, Art Moran and his testimony. Readers relive the scene as Moran remembers it, and only during the cross-examination in Chapter 3 are they reminded that the story is being told by a character on the witness stand and not an omniscient narrator.

This shifting point of view is a technique that Guterson uses effectively throughout his novel to reveal the shaping of the information. Of course, the information available to the reader isn't available to all the characters. Guterson is careful not to reveal the direction of the narrative; instead, he is content to provide tidbits of information that prove to be quite significant— for example, that Carl Heine's grandfather "had established thirty acres of strawberry fields on prime growing land in Center Valley"—as though they were just part of the detailed description.

By the end of the third chapter, it's obvious that the heavy fog, the spare batteries, and the wound on Carl's skull are pivotal pieces of information for the trial, but no mention of motive exists. Neither is there any hint of racism—one of the novel's most important themes. Although the information has yet to be revealed, most of San Piedro's Caucasian population don't consider their neighbors to be Japanese-Americans; they consider them to be Japanese. The memories of World War II are kept alive by all the Americans—Japanese and White—on San Piedro.

(Here and in the following sections, difficult words and phrases are explained.)

- **salmon gill-netters** fishermen who used flat nets that suspended vertically in the water to capture fish, especially salmon. The head of the fish passed through the mesh opening, but the fish entangled itself as it attempted to withdraw.

- **crabber** a person who fishes for crabs.

- **halibut schooner** a boat rigged with two or more masts used for fishing halibut.

- **casements** windows with hinges that allow them to open from the inside.

- **Northwest Passage** the water route along the northern coast of North America leading from the Atlantic Ocean to the Pacific Ocean.

- **Nootka** a member of a Wakashan (Native American) people of Vancouver Island and the surrounding region; large timber trees grown on the Pacific Coast of the United States are named after them.

- **purse seiners** large nets designed to be set by two boats around a school of fish and so arranged that after the ends have been brought together the bottom can be closed.

- **chandlery** a retail shop dealing in provisions, supplies, or equipment of a specified kind; in this context, probably a boating supply shop.

- **bracken** clump of ferns with stem and leaves up to four feet high and three feet wide.

- **miasma** a heavy, vaporous atmosphere.

- **the net was all run out** The fishing nets are set in the water, as though in use, although apparently not being used.

- **launch** a small motorboat.

- **coast guard** military coastal patrol set up to enforce navigation laws and to protect life and property at sea.

- **with her net set** Here, "her" refers to the ship *Susan Marie*; the fishing nets were in the water, though apparently not being used; when fishing nets are "all run out," they are said to be "set."

- **set the fenders out** Rubber cushions—"fenders"—are placed between the boat and the dock (or another boat) to protect the boat's body.

- **deck cleats** pieces of metal attached to the boat dock to which rope line can be secured.

- **guys and stays** control ropes.

- **flange** a metal rim for attachment to another object.

- **picking lights** lights used to illuminate the deck of the ship.

- **jacklight** a light used for fishing at night to attract fish.

- **stern-picker** a standard net fishing boat.

- **stern-side entry** an entrance to the cabin on the rear side.

- **abaft of midship** toward the stern of midship.

- **stood to port** stood on the left side.

- **marine battery** a battery that converts stored energy into electrical energy, similar to those used in golf carts; these batteries allow lights to operate without the engine running.

- **his dinghy's over the reel** A dinghy is a small boat often carried on a larger boat and used for emergencies; if it were "over the reel," then it was still spooled on the side of the boat, waiting to be used.

- **transom** the outer-side of the back of a boat.

- **stern gunnel** the back upper edge of a boat.

- **starboard gunnel** the right upper edge of a boat.

- **gunnel roller** a roller attached to the upper edge of the boat, used to raise and lower fishing nets.

CHAPTERS 4–6

An overview of Ishmael's life is presented as the particulars of his involvement with the case are disclosed. An omniscient narrator provides background into Ishmael's character, describing his father ("an unflagging loyalty to his profession and its principles had made Arthur, over the years, increasingly deliberate in his speech and actions, and increasingly exacting regarding the truth"), as well as providing part of the explanation for Ishmael's cynicism toward people and life. Ishmael's character contrasts with the fishermen of San Piedro, though he is as isolated from the other men on the island as the Japanese-Americans are.

Ishmael—the only reporter on the island—who is solely responsible for the *San Piedro Review*, begins to piece together information for his story. A number of fishermen saw Carl Heine early the night before, and a few boats were in the vicinity of the *Susan Marie*, including Miyamoto's *Islander*. Art Moran speaks to Ishmael off-the-record; admitting that he needs to investigate some tricky little facts, the sheriff asks Ishmael to print that Carl's death was an accident.

Horace Whaley, the county coroner, is the next witness to testify. He examined Carl's dead body and noticed a few things during his autopsy—most importantly, that Carl Heine was still breathing when he entered the water. Whaley also noticed a wound to Carl's skull behind the left ear; he mentions his suspicions that the gash was administered by someone trained in the art of *kendo* (stick fighting), suggesting that a Japanese man is guilty of inflicting the wound as he notes, "The majority of Japs . . . inflicted death over the left ear, swinging in from the right." During cross-examination, though, Horace concedes that he couldn't determine whether the wound occurred before or after death, and that Carl's death was due to drowning.

Horace is the first to suggest that a Japanese man was involved with Carl's injury. His suspicions are a combination of the facts and his own history and bias. The unanswered question is "are these racist comments or non-biased facts?" Horace refers to an entire people as "Japs," as did a fisherman who was discussing the incident when Kabuo's boat was mentioned. The fishermen refer to Kabuo by his last name, as a sucker who looks like all the others, or as a Jap; Ishmael is the only one to use Kabuo's first name. Horace also suggested that Art search for "a Jap with a bloody gun butt." His comments upset the sheriff, who considered them an insult.

Though the information about the islanders' racism is overtly provided, vital information for piecing together what happened—like the fact that Ole Jurgensen now owns Carl's father's land—is mentioned in parentheses, almost as an afterthought. As Guterson reveals the separation that exists among the islanders, he's developing an idea about how racism affects the judicial system. Although they live in close physical proximity to one another, the distance between the Whites and the non-Whites is immense.

Sheriff Moran has a difficult time telling Susan Marie Heine about the accident that took her husband's life. Her reaction isn't one that he can anticipate, for after she receives the news, all she is able to say is, "I knew this would happen one day." The sheriff needs to determine whether she's referring to an accident or to murder.

- **parish beadle** a church officer who keeps order during the service.
- **fly boy** a worker whose chief duty is to load and unload the printing presses.
- **bow-picker** a small fishing boat.
- **mooring lines** ropes used to attach a boat to something else.
- **hull plate** a metal plate secured on the front of the floating part of the boat.
- **drag floats** flotation devices used to retard wave motion.

- **duck loads**   charges for firearms, designed especially for ducks.

- **bow gunnel**   the boat's front, upper edge.

- **motor abreast**   to steer a boat beside another.

- **gaff**   a handled hook for holding or lifting heavy fish.

- **piling**   a long slender column used to carry a vertical load.

- **silvers**   the common name of silver salmon, which is prized for its superb taste.

- **fog run**   in foggy conditions, sounding the prescribed signal of one long blast and two short blasts with either a foghorn or a bell every two minutes.

- **fishing scow**   a large, flat-bottomed boat with broad square ends used chiefly for transporting bulk material.

- **ambergris**   used for perfume, these gray secretions come from whale intestines and are found floating on the ocean or the shore.

- **lee of the cabin**   the side sheltered from the wind.

- **fairleads**   rings through which ropes are passed to guide them.

- **stanchion**   an upright post.

CHAPTERS 7 AND 8

Essential information about Hatsue's character is revealed in Chapter 7, first by recounting the general history of the Japanese arriving on San Piedro Island and then by describing the specifics of the arrival of Hatsue's family. Both situations provide insight into what living in an oppressed culture was like. Nameless Japanese immigrants worked in the wood mill on the island; after it closed, strawberries became the immigrants' main source of income. Readers experience the difficult life Hatsue endured as one of five daughters, all of whom worked diligently in the strawberry fields. Her parents were berry farmers who valued both hard work and the traditions of their birth country.

When Hatsue was thirteen, her mother sent her to Mrs. Shigemura for training in the ways of Japanese women, as a reminder that she herself is Japanese and should think of herself that way. Mrs. Shigemura taught Hatsue the Japanese traditions, customs, and beliefs, often by contrasting them to the American culture.

This training provided Hatsue with internal conflicts. Outwardly, she learned to display the tranquility of Japanese culture, but inwardly she yearned for an American lifestyle. Ironically, Hatsue also desired to eliminate this yearning. Hatsue recognized both her Japanese and American influences and wanted to favor her ancestry, but her American influence enabled her to have a high school romance with Ishmael. She grew up with Ishmael, yet because of the their differences, they weren't friends in public, especially during their romance. If American influences enabled Hatsue to have a love affair with Ishmael, then her Japanese influences enabled her to forget him.

Although Hatsue was born and grew up on San Piedro—and thus was an American—she and her family were ushered to Manzanar, an internment camp, with all San Piedro's other residents of Japanese descent after the bombing of Pearl Harbor. At the camp, Hatsue and Kabuo married. Eight days later he left to fight for the Americans in World War II.

During a break in the trial, when Hatsue is talking with Kabuo, she comments on the snowfall. Snow is used not only to mark the passing of time—she tells Kabuo, "A big snow. Your son's first"—but also to segue into memories of Manzanar. In Hatsue's memories, Kabuo isn't mentioned until Manzanar. In the narrative, only after they're married does she recall who he is and why he's a perfect match for her. In Kabuo, Hatsue finds a man who wants what she wants, and although during her first kiss with Kabuo her mind wanders to a memory of Ishmael, her romantic feelings for Ishmael are long dead.

The abruptness of their marriage challenges the reader: Why so quickly? The details about the romance between Ishmael and Hatsue aren't fully revealed yet, and it isn't clear whether this marriage is an action or reaction on Hatsue's behalf. The difficulty in the relationship between Hatsue and Ishmael is determining the extent of investment both parties had in the relationship and who, if anyone, is at fault for the romance's disintegration.

In the courtroom, as Hatsue talks with Kabuo, Ishmael observes Hatsue's interaction with her husband, and the reporter can't help but remember growing up with Hatsue. Unlike Hatsue,

Ishmael was in love and was determined to keep that feeling forever. Ishmael fondly remembers their first kiss, and then the second, years later. He recalls how Hatsue avoided him, so he ended up spying on her. Finally, he followed her into the woods, to a hollow cedar where they played together years earlier—a site that would again become their meeting place, this time as high school sweethearts.

In that tree Hatsue encourages Ishmael; she is the one who says, "I'm not sorry about it" when referring to the kiss they shared. But at this time in Hatsue's life, she's torn between two worlds. Hatsue needs to experience an American relationship as a way to fully experience both cultures. During their time together, Hatsue knows that the relationship won't last, using the analogy of an ocean to explain her feelings. When she tells him, "Oceans don't mix," it's no coincidence that she uses color to explain her understanding of the difference—a surface-level reference to skin color, which symbolizes their greater cultural differences.

Ishmael, in contrast, claims, "It's all really just one ocean," yet even during their romance, Ishmael and Hatsue didn't mix at school or in the berry fields. In both locations they don't even acknowledge one another's presence. And he accepts that. Chapters 7 and 8 provide the contrasts that affect Hatsue and Ishmael—not only during their romance but also for the rest of their lives. Hatsue is the one who questions whether their relationship may be wrong. Neither she nor Ishmael say whether they think their association is wrong, but they do concede that their friends and parents wouldn't approve. Instead of answering the question outright, they kiss. And Ishmael decided to "love Hatsue forever no matter what came to pass" and does just that. He inaccurately "felt certain Hatsue felt the same way."

Ishmael never really knew Hatsue; readers, however, get inside her mind, a place Ishmael can never access. She wants Kabuo, but she also needs him. Kabuo would provide for her the life of "composure and tranquility of an island strawberry farmer." Hatsue decided that she needed a purpose in her life and a purpose in her love. As a result, she married Kabuo and chose to lie to him when he asked her whether she had ever kissed someone. Hatsue knew that her loyalty is to her husband, and she assures Kabuo, "You're my only" when he asked whether she'd ever experienced a sexual relationship.

Another problematic aspect of the interracial love story is the fact that Hatsue seemingly makes a logical decision regarding what she wants from life and from a husband; yet, in most Western cultures, love is neither explained nor understood in terms of logic, but rather in terms of emotion. This contrasting understanding of love illustrates the difficulties of pursuing an interracial romance.

In addition to developing the characters of Hatsue and Ishmael, Chapters 7 and 8 also provide insight into the views of the islanders. Even in this post-war period, an unwritten law mandates that the Japanese sit in the rear of the courthouse. During the war, most islanders felt that the "exiling of the Japanese was the right thing to do" because "there was a war on and that changed everything." But even before the war, the census takers and mill operators didn't record any of the Japanese by name. Instead they used a numbering system to refer to bodies and not people; attitudes didn't really change. The common perception among the majority of White islanders was that the Japanese were on San Piedro to be used as long as they were useful. In general, even though they were hard workers, those of Japanese descent were neither trusted nor respected.

- **schooner hands** members of the ship's crew.
- **baishakunin** a person who procured homeland brides for Japanese men who lived in the United States.
- **hakujin** Japanese term for Caucasians.
- **schottische** a round dance resembling a slow polka.
- **brigands** bandits.
- **bacchanal** drunken revelry.
- **potlatch** a social event.
- **Tojo** a celebrated Japanese general of World War II.
- **odori** a traditional Japanese dance.
- **utsukushii** beautiful.

- **geoduck clams**   edible clams, sometimes weighing over five pounds.
- **barnacles**   difficult-to-remove marine shellfish that attach to rocks, ship bottoms, and other surfaces.
- **siphon**   the tubular organ used for drawing in or ejecting fluids.
- **alder stick**   a branch from a tree in the birch family.
- **transits**   an instrument with a mounted telescope used for measuring angles.
- **alidades**   surveying instruments used for determining direction.
- **pelts**   the skin and fur of an animal.
- **creosote**   the liquid mixture obtained from the heating and cooling of wood tar.
- **nimbus**   a circle of light around the head.
- **dell**   a secluded hollow or small valley.

CHAPTERS 9 AND 10

Chapters 9 and 10 are predominantly the testimony of Etta Heine, Carl's mother, but Guterson reveals more to the reader than to the jurors. In both the present and in flashback, telling information about deals and attitudes is revealed. Etta took the witness stand, providing the information that potentially explained the motive Kabuo may have had for killing Carl. Etta testifies that while Carl junior was away at war, his father died, and Etta sold the farm to Ole Jurgensen.

Etta remembers, during a trial recess, how Zenhichi Miyamoto, Kabuo's father, approached Carl Sr. with an offer to purchase seven acres of land. Etta was opposed from the onset, stating firmly, "'We ain't going to sell.'" Readers soon come to find that although Etta claims to be against the sale because the land will be worth more later, in actuality she didn't like or trust the Japanese man.

On the stand, Etta speaks as more than the deceased's mother: She is the embodiment of the majority of San Piedro. She's speaking for them, the majority who are suspicious of those who are different and feel superior to the Japanese (and the Indians). The differences are both cultural and socioeconomical. The migrants are the working class who are viewed as a group and not as individuals. On San Piedro, these groups were worthy to work the land, not to own it.

Disregarding his wife's opinion, Carl Sr. did agree to an eight-year, lease-to-own contract. Laws at that time prevented aliens from owning land and other laws prevented Japanese from becoming naturalized citizens, so in essence it was impossible for Zenhichi to own land. Carl couldn't legally sell it to him even though he wanted to do so. Another law prevented Carl from holding the land for Zenhichi. With Carl agreeing to hold the lease, the arrangement they devised didn't break the law, although it did bend it a good bit. After the last payment was made, Carl would deed the land to Zenhichi's oldest son, Kabuo. Etta testifies "'The law let 'em own land if they were citizens. Them Miyamoto kids were born here so they're citizens, I guess.'" Ironically, even though Bavarian-born Etta is a citizen only through her marriage to Carl, she is reluctant to concede citizenship to those born in the United States.

Carl didn't share the same racist views as his wife, telling Etta "'it don't make one bit of difference which way it is their eyes slant. . . . People is people, comes down to it. And these are clean-living people. Nothing wrong with them.'" When Carl read about the internment of the Japanese, he knew that islanders would take advantage of their neighbors. Etta's first thought when she heard about the upcoming internment was about the lack of pickers this year and the need to get some Chinamen to do the work. Carl and Etta's contrasting views illustrate the fact that not all of the islanders were racist; however, for the most part, those who weren't didn't speak up. Carl's intention was to help Zenhichi, which he told him. Etta only remembers the conversation; she doesn't testify about it. In Etta's mind, as in the mind of many racists, ambiguity is nonexistent: She was convinced Carl's intention wasn't legal, and when Carl died, his good intentions were buried with him.

Etta testifies that the Miyamotos missed the last two payments on the agreement. In Etta's eyes, two missed payments, along with the fact that Japanese couldn't own land anyway, were reason enough to sell the land to someone else. As she testifies, Judge Fielding attempts to maintain order and have Etta comment only on the facts of the case; however, she's determined to speak her mind, and although remarks may be stricken from the record, the jury still heard her say, "They've been botherin' us over those seven acres for near ten years now. My son was killed over it."

Etta is convinced that Carl's former high school friend killed her son, but because she never considered Kabuo a suitable friend for Carl Jr., she doesn't even remember his name. Etta does remember making her son return the bamboo fishing rod he was given as the Miyamotos prepared to leave for Manzanar. She needed her son to make this gesture because she needed her son's opinion to be more like hers than like his father's. As she sends him back with the rod, she thinks, "The boy was not all Carl's. Her son, too, she felt that."

The sale of the land occurs while Carl, Jr. is away at war. Although the war puts a strain on Carl and Kabuo's friendship, the reader never gets the impression that the men hate each other. However, Etta uses her influence on her son to make him suspicious of Kabuo and his motives. She testifies that her son "'said he'd have to keep an eye out for Kabuo.'"

Under cross-examination, Etta concedes that the difference between the price the Miyamoto family would have paid and the price Ole Jurgensen did pay was a $2,500 increase. For Etta this situation was win/win: The Japs didn't own her land, and she increased her profit.

Etta's flashbacks enable readers to know more fully the facts of the situation—at least the facts from Etta's point of view. With this knowledge, readers can compare the entirety of the story with the court testimony, deciding how what isn't mentioned in court— but is actually pertinent information—affects the fairness of the way that the judicial system works. This extra information also enables readers to determine the reliability of Etta's testimony. It also betrays the grave prejudices Etta feels toward those not like her. She's glad to see the Japanese sent to internment camps as she tells her husband. "'They're Japs . . . We're in a war with them. We can't have spies around.'"

Ole's testimony is that of a person who doesn't want to get involved. Although he testifies that he wasn't aware of any claim by Miyamoto to seven acres of land, in the next breath he admits, "I bring it up with Etta, you see. . . . I know seven acres has been sold to them." Ole accepts Etta's explanation, questioning her no further.

Not only did Ole know that the Miyamotos were living on the land (he purchased their house, too, when he bought the land), but he also knew that they were living in an internment camp but "'maybe they won' come b-back.'" Curiously, Ole's conscience is eased when Etta tells him that she intends to return the Miyamoto's money.

After Kabuo returned from the war, he questioned Ole about the seven acres of land; Ole sent him to speak to Etta. Answering Etta's explanation of the events that transpired, Kabuo responded, "You haven't done anything illegal. Wrong is a different matter." Kabuo's statement is one of the major themes of *Snow Falling on Cedars*: the relationship between legality and morality in determining right and wrong.

Kabuo speaks of a higher authority than a law—he's speaking of a moral law or code of conduct. Codes of conduct affect cultures, regions, and professions. These unwritten rules govern the actions of those who follow them. The problem with moral codes is the ambiguity that exists in many situations, as well as the potential for conflict between cultures, and thus a conflict in codes of conduct.

Later on in his testimony, in another seemingly throwaway line, Ole Jurgensen remembers seeing Kabuo swinging a wooden sword in the field, echoing Art Moran's earlier testimony that he suspected someone trained in kendo to have been involved with Carl's death. Mentioning this detail foreshadows revelations yet to come.

The final part of Ole Jurgensen's testimony is about agreeing to sell the land back to Carl Jr. and Kabuo's reaction to this news. Kabuo's reaction was understandable. He missed out on an opportunity to reclaim what he considered his family's land, and worse, the man who agreed to purchase the land is an immediate relative of the woman who cheated Kabuo's family. Ole's wife phoned Carl and told him that Kabuo had been by. When Carl goes to the farm to take down the For Sale sign, Ole tells him about the meeting in great detail. He then testifies that "Carl Heine nodded again and again and then came down from the ladder with the sign. 'Thanks for telling me,' he'd said." The reader is left to guess at what this big, quiet man was thinking as he listened to Ole's narrative. Nine days after Jurgensen accepts Carl Jr.'s earnest money, Carl is found dead.

• **sciatica**   pain in the lower back.

- **anteroom** an outer room that leads to another usually more important room and is often used as a waiting area.
- **chuck** an inlet.
- **sea-run cutthroat** a desirable species of trout.
- **trolling** fishing by pulling a line through the water.
- **ferrules** rings put around a slender shaft to strengthen it and prevent it from splitting.

CHAPTER 11

Until now, readers have experienced Kabuo only as the jurors and courtroom observers have seen him—silent and stoic. What readers know of Kabuo has been revealed from Hatsue's point of view. In Chapter 11, for the first time, events are told from Kabuo's point of view, but they're not the events surrounding Carl's death. Instead, Kabuo remembers the war.

The war—not this trial—is the defining event of Kabuo's life. He, like many other men at Manzanar, had a need to fight for the country that had turned its back on him. Kabuo saw enlisting in the military as a matter of honor. Kabuo views himself as a man who had "forever sacrificed his tranquility in order that they [inhabitants of San Piedro] might have theirs." Islanders don't view him that way, for most see his composure as a sign of defiance. This composure, however, is really Kabuo's cover for raging emotions—anger and guilt—that Kabuo keeps hidden inside.

Kabuo feels guilty because he killed four Germans during the war, with the first one haunting his memories. After the war, Kabuo returned to San Piedro as scarred as every other veteran. Serving in the military was the honorable thing to do, but nonetheless, Kabuo came home considering himself a murderer. He felt the need to atone for his actions and thus longed for punishment and suffering.

Sitting in the courtroom, Kabuo was trying to follow his father's teaching, "the greater the composure, the more revealed was one." Although he was trying to project this demeanor, the people in the courtroom saw something different. Islanders, especially the jurors, didn't trust composure. This misinterpretation of a person's behavior is another example of a cultural conflict.

Another difference between cultures is the manner in which death is treated. The Japanese view of life embraces death rather than fears it. For the most part, Kabuo accepts this philosophy and tries to live accordingly, but when the reality sinks in that Alvin Hooks would seek the death penalty if Kabuo were found guilty of murder, Kabuo does fear death.

After remembering his combat experiences, Kabuo reflects on his relationship with Hatsue. He remembers seeing her in the strawberry fields and in the classroom, loving her from afar. Their relationship developed slowly at Manzanar, but when he found out that they both had the same innermost desires, his feelings moved toward love.

The relationship between Kabuo and Hatsue illustrates the differences between cultures in the way love is viewed. Kabuo falls in love with Hatsue for different reasons than Ishmael. Love is secondary to honor because honor defines who a person is; Kabuo and Hatsue loved each other for who they were, even though for Kabuo this meant he had to enlist in the army. If Kabuo did not enlist, then he wasn't being true to himself. And if he were not true to himself, he wouldn't be worthy of Hatsue. Kabuo falls in love with Hatsue because, ultimately, they have the same goals and dreams. Their love was based on mutual respect and understanding. Kabuo didn't spend nearly the amount of time with Hatsue as Ishmael did, but that issue wasn't important to him.

A very significant point revealed during Kabuo's memories is that Hatsue asked Kabuo to marry her. She initiated their union, knowing full well that he was leaving. Hatsue makes this decision, which may have been made in haste, as a means for helping her get over Ishmael. She also may have made the decision because she finally knows what she wants.

Kabuo's final memories are of his training at age seven with the kendo stick. His great-grandfather was a samurai. Kabuo practiced in the fields before going to work. He would practice all of his moves, including "the most common of kendo strokes, a horizontal thrust a right-handed man could propel with great force against the left side of his enemy's head." Kabuo is right-handed. After the war, his stick still provided him solace and comfort, and he practices in the fields late at night as a way of trying to deal with his guilt.

- **katana** a curved Japanese sword worn by samurais with the edge up.
- **scabbard** the sheath for a sling sword; for Japanese aristocracy, this item was often highly decorated.
- **kendo** a bamboo or wooden stick used for the Japanese sport of fencing.
- **sageo** a personal flag.
- **obi** a belt, or sash.
- **hakama** pleated trousers that appear to be a skirt.
- **bokken** a curved wooden sword.
- **dojo** an exercise hall.
- **zenshin** constant awareness of impending danger.
- **samurai** the warrior aristocracy of Japan.
- **Meiji restoration** the return of the imperial family in 1867 as rulers of Japan after the overthrow of the shogun; this period changed the feudal state into an industrialized and Westernized nation and brought about the abolition of samurai.
- **Great Wheel** a symbol for all life, circulating and rotating throughout time.

CHAPTERS 12 AND 13

In Chapters 12 and 13, Guterson describes life on San Piedro immediately following the attack on Pearl Harbor. Ishmael and Hatsue had been carrying on a secret romance for four years, but during their senior year, before the bombing of Pearl Harbor, Hatsue was beginning to verbalize to Ishmael her doubts about their liaison. Hatsue believed that her actions in this life affected future lives, and she seemed certain that she would suffer for her deceitful ways; however, Hatsue was not so distraught that she stopped seeing Ishmael.

After the bombing of Pearl Harbor, the islanders of San Piedro were divided, with the majority of the Caucasians taking an "us versus them" stance. The "us," of course, were Americans, who were against the Japanese. The day after the bombing, Ishmael's father reported in two separate articles that "the island's Japanese community pledged their loyalty to the United States," and he emphasized in his editorial the need to remain calm.

This editorial closed with another major theme of *Snow Falling on Cedars*: "prejudice and hatred are never right and [are] never to be accepted by a just society." Yet justice, especially during wartime, is difficult at best. Arthur Chambers tried to balance the news he printed by pointing out the positive things that the members of the island's Japanese community did for the United States, and he was accused of showing favoritism. Subscribers and advertisers alike began to cancel their affiliation with the *San Piedro Review*, though Arthur was confident that he and the paper could survive without them.

In order to understand the attitudes and resentment of the inhabitants of San Piedro during the time of Kabuo's trial, it's imperative to see how the islanders reacted to the bombing of Pearl Harbor and how they treated their neighbors immediately after that. Their public comments, their actions, and their letters to the editor display the hostility, resentment, and fear they felt. And fear is a powerful emotion. When people are ruled by fear, reasoning with them is impossible. Reason is logical, but the only thing that will overcome an emotion like fear is a stronger emotion, like hate. Reasoning with a racist, therefore, is likewise impossible because racism isn't logical. Unfortunately, especially for the Japanese-Americans, many Americans tended to override logic with emotion, oftentimes with disturbing results.

Guterson uses snow in these chapters to describe how in the present everything is being covered and blinded. And in the time period immediately following the bombing of Pearl Harbor, most inhabitants of San Piedro were blinded by their emotions. The swirling snow in the present narrows one's vision, just as the many narrow-minded inhabitants were blanketed in fear and distrust.

- **eviscerated**   deprived of force.
- **boilerplate**   unoriginal, standard.
- **alder**   small birch trees that grow best in wet ground.
- **saboteurs**   persons destroying enemy war materials.

- **reconnaissance**   gathering information about position, strength, and movement of enemy troops.

- **gunny bag**   a bag made from a coarse, heavy hemp material.

CHAPTER 14

Chapter 14 chronicles the turning point in Hatsue's life. After her father is arrested, Hatsue and her mother have an important conversation. Hatsue doesn't know the extent of her mother's knowledge, but clearly Hatsue's attempts to conceal her relationship with Ishmael during the past four years haven't been entirely successful.

Hatsue benefits from the wisdom of her mother. Even as Hatsue speaks out, contradicting what her mother says to her, Hatsue knows that her mother is a living example of how a Japanese woman is expected to live. Fujiko verbalizes a major difference between Japanese and American cultures. This difference deals with the notion and understanding of the ego. Fujiko believes, as do many Japanese, that the individual is a significant part of a greater whole, and therefore, emphasis is not placed on any one person. In contrast, many Americans believe that their individuality—what separates them from all others—is essential to their understanding of self.

Fujiko is a positive, maternal role model in *Snow Falling on Cedars*. Same-sex parental role models play an important part in character development. Kabuo and Ishmael each had a father whose examples and attitudes they could follow as they matured, and although Hatsue learned from Mrs. Shigemura the ways of the Japanese culture, Hatsue learned how to be a Japanese woman from her mother.

Hatsue is understandably torn between two worlds—"her instincts did not make the kinds of distinctions having Japanese blood demanded"—but the aftermath of the bombing of Pearl Harbor is forcing Hatsue to decide who she is. When she verbalizes her reaction, her mother demonstrates through actions and words that sometimes it is better not to speak—a connection Hatsue immediately makes to the silence she has been keeping about her romance.

38

After her father is arrested, Hatsue has to start considering herself either American or Japanese, and she initially favors the country of her birth. But Fujiko reminds Hatsue of her blood and her upbringing, leaving Hatsue more confused than ever. As she puzzles over her Japanese heritage and her illicit romance with Ishmael, she thinks "If identity was geography instead of blood—if living in a place was what really mattered—then Ishmael was a part of her . . . as much as anything Japanese."

Hatsue remains torn and confused as she and Ishmael prepare to deal with their separation, for she knows that the Japanese-Americans will be moved from the island. The day before they are separated, they share a moment as one. Ironically, the moment Ishmael is physically closest to Hatsue—penetration during inter-course—also results in the moment that he is farthest from her spiritually. "No, Ishmael, no Ishmael, never," she told him as she pushed him away from and out of her.

Hatsue is clearly no longer interested in pursuing a romantic relationship with Ishmael. What is not so clear is the reason why. Is Hatsue choosing her ancestry over her present-day life? Is she reacting to the problems in the world? Or is she merely taking the easy way out? Is Hatsue afraid of taking a chance with Ishmael, a *hakujin*? How readers answer the preceding questions determines how Hatsue is viewed as a character. In order for Hatsue to be a sympathetic character, she has to be making a tough decision that she truly feels is the correct one.

- **shakuhachi** a bamboo flute.
- **kimono** a loose robe that fastens with a wide sash.
- **stevedores** persons who load and unload cargo ships.
- **vole** a short-tailed, mouselike rodent.
- **salal** a small shrub of the Pacific Coast, having edible dark purple berries about the size of a common grape.

CHAPTER 15

Chapter 15 is narrated from Fujiko's point of view, chronicling the time she and her daughters spent being transported to and living at Manzanar. Fujiko notices the islanders who watch those of

Japanese descent who had not been arrested—namely the women and children—board the ferry, but she refuses to acknowledge them. During the transport, Fujiko refuses to speak of her own discomfort because she tries to model for her daughters what she considers to be appropriate behavior.

This chapter describes the treatment of Japanese-Americans at Manzanar. Again, specific details—like having to wash in a trough but being given no soap—make the scene come alive. Living conditions at best are difficult, but the inhabitants don't complain too much; they survive the best that they can.

Fujiko intercepts and reads Ishmael's letter to Hatsue. Fujiko, understandably upset, forces herself to "behave with dignity" as she confronts her daughter. Fujiko claims Hatsue has been deceiving both her mother and herself. Much of Fujiko's rage stems from the fact that thoughts of romance are not a part of Fujiko's own life. She, herself, was deceived with her arranged marriage. Fujiko ended up learning to live with her husband, and "she found that she had learned to love him, if love was the proper word to use, and it occurred to her then . . . that love was nothing close to what she'd imagined. . . . It was less dramatic and far more practical than her girlhood had led her to believe." Thus, Fujiko's marriage is a result of her conscious decision to stay married to Hisao—not out of any sort of romantic love.

In an effort to help her daughter and herself bring closure to the interracial relationship, Fujiko writes a letter to Ishmael's parents. After Hatsue reads the letter, her mother allows her to write her own instead. Later, Fujiko invites Kabuo to stay for tea after he brings a chest of drawers to their room. Soon he asks Hatsue to go for a walk. A few months later, Hatsue agrees to see Kabuo because she can't "grieve over Ishmael Chambers until the end of her days." Hatsue is grieving over the loss of a relationship or the loss of Ishmael, or perhaps a little of both. As she gets to know Kabuo, she realizes that she admires him and that they both have similar dreams; however, during their first kiss, she remembers Ishmael.

Guterson uses this chapter to interweave character and plot development with social commentary. Many Americans know little, if anything, about the internment of Japanese-Americans during World War II. Oftentimes, people who are outraged about the concentration camps in Germany never condemn the atrocities committed against Americans by Americans during the same war.

Guterson's style enables him to expose readers to the difficulties experienced by those in the camp without having to be didactic or preachy. A detailed description about the conditions of Manzanar provide all the commentary Guterson needs to illustrate his point of view. This chapter also effectively portrays the difficulties of being a Japanese woman living in an American culture, a difficulty that is passed from generation to generation.

- **typhoid** a bacterial infection resulting in severe intestinal disturbances and rose-red spots on the chest and abdomen.

- **giri** doing what is expected or required, without emotion or response.

CHAPTER 16

Once again, Ishmael's experience with a situation is contrasted with Hatsue's. Just as Hatsue spends her time during the war putting Ishmael out of her life, he spends his time hating her. His service as a marine led him to a hospital and then to an ill-planned invasion mission. Having spent the five months since Hatsue's letter arrived in an emotional hell, Ishmael now experiences a physical one, too. This is a chapter of losses for Ishmael—loss of a division, loss of an arm, and loss of a woman. Through these losses, Ishmael suffers on a variety of levels. His physical loss (his arm) and his emotional loss (his relationship with Hatsue) intertwine, leaving Ishmael scarred both literally and figuratively.

With enough details of blood and guts, Guterson fairly easily describes the physical pain; however, capturing the pain of a broken heart is a bit more difficult. Guterson achieves success, though, by allowing Ishmael to spend time sick and alone. When Ishmael is encouraged to write a final letter home, he addresses it to Hatsue and tells her how much he hates her. He never mails the letter. His anger toward her and the way that she treated him is clear, and by the end of the chapter, he refers to Hatsue as "that fucking goddamn Jap bitch."

By contrasting points of view, Guterson prevents either character—Ishmael or Hatsue—from being viewed solely in a positive or negative light. Instead, he reveals the complexity of the situation by providing insight into both characters. Perhaps neither character is to blame for the way events leading to their separation transpired, but the notion that neither is blameless for the aftermath is too pat and too simplistic. The characters don't take responsibility for their actions (or lack thereof), and by avoiding the issues and one another, they harbor feelings of hate and indifference. Avoiding an unpleasant situation won't make it go away; on the surface level, this attitude applies to Ishmael and Hatsue; on a deeper level, this attitude applies to all the Caucasians and the Japanese inhabitants of San Piedro.

- **frigates**   sailing war vessels of medium size.
- **daisy cutters**   slang for anti-personnel bombs.
- **coxswain**   a person who steers a small boat.
- **seawall**   an embankment used to prevent the erosion of the shore.

CHAPTERS 17 AND 18

Chapters 17 and 18 focus on the trial. Sheriff Moran's testimony for the second time speculates that Kabuo tied the *Islander* (his boat) to Carl's boat and then made a quick getaway. In his haste, Kabuo inadvertently switched one of his lines with Carl's. The sheriff has five concerns that, when taken together, enable him to get a search warrant for Kabuo's boat to search for a murder weapon. During his search, Sheriff Moran finds a long-handled gaff with blood on both ends and arrests Kabuo, who has already declared his innocence.

Moran's testimony starts to solidify the prosecution's case. The information provided in his testimony may provide enough evidence—the means, the motive, and the method—for the jury to find Kabuo guilty. As the sheriff is arresting Kabuo, he notices the eyes of the accused and is convinced that Kabuo's eyes are concealing emotions; Sheriff Moran believes that the look in Kabuo's eyes mean that he is "hiding something," probably the truth.

Describing the weather during the afternoon of the trial, Guterson uses snow to comment on the attitudes of most San Piedro inhabitants. For the most part, the islanders are more accepting of the precipitation than they are of people. They prepare

42

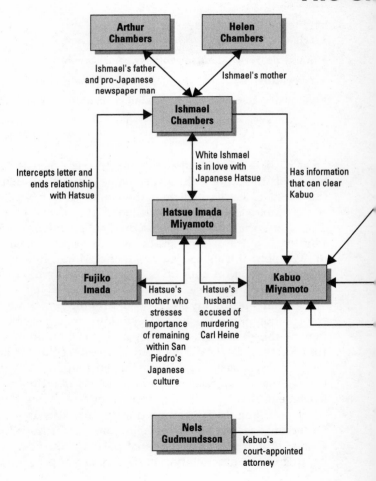

Arthur Chambers

Helen Chambers

Ishmael's father and pro-Japanese newspaper man

Ishmael's mother

Ishmael Chambers

Intercepts letter and ends relationship with Hatsue

White Ishmael is in love with Japanese Hatsue

Has information that can clear Kabuo

Hatsue Imada Miyamoto

Fujiko Imada

Hatsue's mother who stresses importance of remaining within San Piedro's Japanese culture

Hatsue's husband accused of murdering Carl Heine

Kabuo Miyamoto

Nels Gudmundsson

Kabuo's court-appointed attorney

aracters

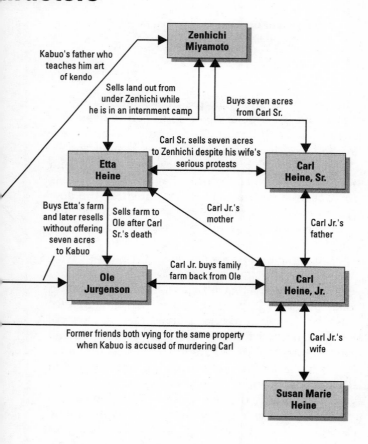

Zenhichi Miyamoto

Kabuo's father who teaches him art of kendo

Sells land out from under Zenhichi while he is in an internment camp

Buys seven acres from Carl Sr.

Carl Sr. sells seven acres to Zenhichi despite his wife's serious protests

Etta Heine

Carl Heine, Sr.

Buys Etta's farm and later resells without offering seven acres to Kabuo

Sells farm to Ole after Carl Sr.'s death

Carl Jr.'s mother

Carl Jr.'s father

Ole Jurgenson

Carl Jr. buys family farm back from Ole

Carl Heine, Jr.

Former friends both vying for the same property when Kabuo is accused of murdering Carl

Carl Jr.'s wife

Susan Marie Heine

for the worst, not knowing whether the storm will last three hours or three days, but they do not pretend to know, because the outcome is "out of their control." When dealing with snowfall, islanders prepare for the worst, hope for the best, and accept what comes; in contrast, when the islanders view Japanese-Americans, they prepare for and expect the worst and refuse to see the best.

- **tire chains** chains wrapped around an automobile tire and used in the winter for traction.
- **bowline** a rope on the front of the boat used to keep the weather edge of a vessel's square sail forward when sailing.

CHAPTER 19

During the second day of the trial, the prosecution brings in experts who testify about the type of blood found on the gaff and about Kabuo's experience with kendo. Dr. Whitman, a hematologist, testifies that the blood found on the gaff was human and B-positive. Carl Heine's blood type is B-positive, but Kabuo Miyamoto's is not. The doctor also testifies that the blood type is extremely rare for Caucasians. Under cross-examination, the doctor admits that he doesn't know how the blood got on the handle and does agree that it is more likely to have come from the hand than from the head of Carl Heine. He also is forced to admit that a larger percentage of Japanese males are B-positive than Caucasians.

After local fishermen testify that a fisherman does not board another man's boat unless it is an emergency, Sergeant Maples from the Army testifies. Sergeant Maples trained men in hand-to-hand combat and remembered Kabuo Miyamoto. In fact, Kabuo had taught Sergeant Maples the art of kendo, and Sergeant Maples testifies that Kabuo could indeed defeat a man who was larger than himself, especially if Kabuo's opponent had no kendo training.

The narrative moves quickly through Chapter 19, as quickly as the prosecution is moving through its case. Evidence against Kabuo is mounting, though it is not damning, yet. The pacing of Guterson's narrative increases because the trial is nearing its climax, and the prosecution is presenting a convincing case.

- **hematology** the study of blood and its diseases.

- **topography** the physical features of a region.

- **backing net off his drum** turning the metal cylinder around which the net is wound.

- **lead line** the weighted bottom of a gill net.

- **cork line** a float on the top of a gill net that keeps the net on the surface of the water.

- **Purple Heart** a military decoration of honor for those wounded in action against the enemy.

- **European Theater** the European location where World War II took place.

- **culling** cutting and collecting.

- **froe** a cleaving tool for splitting staves.

CHAPTERS 20 AND 21

Chapters 20 and 21 are the memories and testimony of Carl's widow, Susan Marie. She is strategically placed as the last witness because Alvin Hooks knows how the jury will respond: "The men especially would not wish to betray such a woman with a not-guilty verdict at the end of things." The prosecution will rest its case after Susan Marie's testimony. At first, instead of direct testimony, readers experience Susan Marie's memories. Basically, Carl Heine and Susan Marie had a marriage based on sex. Susan Marie viewed Carl and herself as a good match and considered her husband a good father.

Susan Marie's memories also provide readers with a portrait of Carl Heine. Carl was "silent and dependable," a man who worked nights fishing and took care of his family during the day. Ever since the war, Carl was unable to speak to anyone, especially about important things. The most Susan Marie could get Carl to admit to was that he and Kabuo were friends before the war.

Under cross-examination, Susan Marie admits to Nels Gudmundsson that most of her testimony was hearsay. Because her husband is dead and cannot speak for himself, this testimony is admissible. Her testimony again raises the notion of right and wrong. The conflict between legality and morality is forefront in these chapters, as well as a major theme of *Snow Falling on Cedars*. The examples Guterson presents are not so cut and dry, so black and white, which is the exact point he is trying to make about judging situations. Susan Marie can testify only about what she saw and what she heard, but she didn't hear everything that passed between her husband and Kabuo.

Their wartime experiences affected Carl and Kabuo in similar manners. Although these experiences had a profound impact on their lives, they weren't able to share their feelings about their experiences with their wives, nor were they able to consider each other friends. Before the war, the differences in their races didn't matter; after the war, their differences defined them. Carl and Kabuo illustrate the similarities between cultures and the way that similar situations affect dissimilar individuals.

- **neurasthenia** a condition resulting in fatigue, depression, and headaches.
- **wattle** fleshy folds of skin under the chin.

CHAPTER 22

A snowstorm shuts down the entire island as the prosecution rests its case, and Guterson uses Chapter 22 to illustrate how islanders react to the weather, as well as to provide striking similarities between the primary male characters. Although this chapter doesn't further the plot much—Ishmael's speaking with Hatsue is the highlight—Guterson uses the weather to advance important aspects of character and thematic development, as well as to develop aspects of symbolism.

Ed Soames thinks to himself that "the boy [Ishmael] was not someone you could speak to," and thus Ishmael, like Carl and Kabuo, is a veteran who returns to San Piedro unable to talk after the war. Ironically, Ishmael earns his living through his words. Ishmael also wants to feel the pain where his arm used to be, just as Kabuo wants to suffer for the offenses he committed during the war.

After court is recessed for the day, Ishmael's reporter's instincts take over, and he is out taking pictures of the storm and its effects for the paper because the damage that the storm inflicted on the island is definitely newsworthy. Ishmael's decision to talk to Charlie Toval before running a picture of what may be his run-down, overturned car provides insight into Ishmael's character. Ishmael doesn't want to embarrass Charlie Toval. This detail, almost an afterthought, reveals that Ishmael, though his manner often suggests otherwise, is not entirely uncaring.

The fallen snow removed the borders between property, and no one can distinguish differences below the surface. This covering is a commentary on people and their differences. Ishmael ponders two questions: Do people really fight over land and borders? And, do people really kill for them? Of course, the answer is yes. These are some of the fundamental questions of warfare.

The snow in this chapter is beautiful yet deadly and serves as a metaphor for Hatsue, or at least Ishmael's perception of her. During his wanderings, Ishmael encounters the Imadas and offers them a ride. In the car, Ishmael tries to read Hatsue's eyes. Hatsue talks about Kabuo's trial being unfair, but Ishmael uses her words to strike at her for what she did to him: "You're right—people don't have to be unfair."

Ishmael believes that Hatsue was unfair to him for not giving their relationship a chance to work. Now he realizes that the trial and his newspaper may provide him the means back into Hatsue's life. Gradually his anger toward Hatsue had "dried up and blown away," yet nothing took its place. Perhaps, Ishmael muses, if Kabuo is taken from Hatsue in a manner similar to the way Hatsue was taken from him, she may find her way back into his life. This notion sets the stage for an important decision that Ishmael will have to make.

- **propitious**   advantageous.
- **séance**   a spiritualist meeting to receive spirit communications.
- **solicitous**   meticulously careful.
- **machete**   a large-bladed, heavy knife.

CHAPTER 23

Wanting to research weather records for a newspaper article, Ishmael makes his way to the lighthouse. What he finds there makes Chapter 23 a pivotal point in the narrative. Although the chapter is short, the combination of flashback and finding sets the stage for the climax of the novel.

While at the lighthouse, Ishmael remembers the difficulties he and Hatsue had when they happened to run into each other on the island immediately after the war. His memories trigger action in the present, so Ishmael searches for meaningful information. Although Ishmael came to the lighthouse for information about the weather, he ends up searching for information about the night in question. Ishmael's search leads him to the truth: A freighter threw a wall of water powerful enough to knock a man overboard; that's what happened to Carl. The radiomen who worked that night left the next day, so they know nothing about Carl's death and Kabuo's trial. Revealing this critical information so early moves *Snow Falling on Cedars* from the realm of just being a court-room drama. Of course, this information doesn't explain the entire specifics of the evening, but it is enough to provide reasonable doubt. Because the reader knows the truth, the narrative becomes an exploration of the decision-making process. What will Ishmael do with this information?

Ishmael, thrust into a powerful position, now needs to deal with a plethora of emotions: revenge, spite, hate, love, and ambivalence. He has information unknown to anyone else, and he also has just had a miserable reunion with Hatsue in addition to remembering their awkward, first, post-war meeting. To an outsider, the decision is easy: Ishmael should reveal what he knows. But Ishmael isn't an outsider. He was actively involved with Hatsue and then passively involved with Kabuo's trial, and he can now be actively involved again. From Ishmael's point of view, what is right for Kabuo may not be what is right for himself. Ishmael knows the truth, but knowledge without action is equivalent to ignorance.

- **mail steamers** small ships, propelled by steam, used for mail delivery.

- **timber schooner**   ship used to transport timber.
- **freighter**   ship used to carry cargo.
- **four-masted bark**   a small sailing ship.
- **sounding boards**   safety structures used to extend sound and help ships determine their course when weather conditions are poor.
- **dogleg**   a bent course, named because it resembles a hind leg of a dog.

CHAPTER 24

The first part of this chapter is significant for what Ishmael does *not* do: He does not tell his mother, he does not go to the judge, and he does not do anything at all about the information. Ishmael needs to decide what to do, and while he is deciding, he takes some kerosene and groceries to his mother.

Discussions with his mother about God and about getting over the war not only characterize their relationship but also provide the basis for additional thematic and character developments. The notion of God and whether one exists calls to mind the issue of free will versus fate. Cultural differences about the makeup of God and Ishmael's own ambivalence toward a supreme being do not prevent a god from actually existing. And as Ishmael verbalizes his own traumas and inability to "get over" the war, he is explaining the exact condition Kabuo is in, as Kabuo attempts to deal with his own war-driven guilt.

Twice during their conversation Ishmael asks his mother to "tell me what to do." She thinks he is talking about the unhappiness in his life and encourages him to get married and have children. Ishmael may be referring to that aspect of his life, but more pressingly, he is concerned about the notes in his pocket. Unknowingly, his mother, who feels that "they arrested him [Kabuo] because he's Japanese" may be leading Ishmael in a direction she would not mean to lead him: If Ishmael views not doing anything with the notes as the best means to get Hatsue back in his life, then he may do nothing.

Trying to decide what to do, he re-reads Hatsue's breakup letter, and readers get to see its contents for the first time. The letter is honest and forthright and casts Hatsue in a fairly positive light. For Ishmael, the letter serves as a reminder that the brief moment of sexual intimacy was a culmination of opposites for them. For him, it was confirmation of everything that was right; for Hatsue, it was confirmation of everything that was wrong.

Ishmael decides to write the article Hatsue wants in order to make her "beholden to him." He acknowledges that this is not what his father would do, but he is not his father. Ishmael plans on using the paper to his advantage and to keep the records in his pocket.

Sitting alone in the cold room, Ishmael imagines how he will approach Hatsue after the trial, and readers have to imagine that Ishmael may keep the information to himself.

- **kindling**   small pieces of wood used to start a fire.

- **agnostic**   a person who holds the view that any ultimate reality (as God) is unknown and probably unknowable.

- **Belleau Wood**   an area in northern France that was the site of a violent two-week battle during World War I; the area is now a memorial to soldiers in the United States armed forces who were war casualties.

- **tin lizzie**   slang for a Ford Model T automobile.

- **Bendix**   a radio built by U.S. inventor Vincent Bendix.

- **rice paper**   delicate paper made from rice straw.

CHAPTERS 25 AND 26

In Chapters 25 and 26, the defense presents its case. Hatsue is the first witness, but before she testifies, she remembers how her life changed because of the war. The plans she made with Kabuo weren't realized; she was now living with a man who was living with the memories and demons of the war. For nine years he worked, trying to save money and to figure out a way to buy back his family's land. And Hatsue stood by his side.

Her testimony provides a twist—for the first time, mention is made of a dead battery and that Carl agreed to sell the land to Kabuo. To the spectators and the jurors, this comes as an unexpected and almost unbelievable claim. To the readers who know the truth, the news is equally unexpected but believable.

Under cross-examination, Hatsue gives testimony that is ridiculed and called into question by Alvin Hooks. Keeping silent for three months about news that her husband was indeed aboard Carl's boat is somewhat suspicious. Keeping silent for three months about news that her husband was about to be able to purchase the long-desired land is incredible. Alvin Hooks summarizes and trivializes her testimony by ending with the comment, "I don't know what to believe and what not to believe."

Alvin doesn't need to call Hatsue a liar in order to plant ideas in the minds of the jurors. From his point of view, the route that Hatsue and Kabuo chose to take doesn't make much sense. Alvin is equally adept at using the testimony of Mr. Gillanders, another defense witness, against Kabuo.

Mr. Gillanders, the president of the San Piedro Gill-Netters Association, testifies regarding the code of salmon fishermen. He talks about the fact that a salmon fisherman would board another's boat only during a time of emergency. This testimony corroborates Hatsue's claims. Unfortunately, Alvin Hooks presents an equally plausible theory about tying and boarding another's boat. Alvin asks whether it were possible for Kabuo to feign an emergency as a means to lure Carl to the *Islander*.

This third day of the trial could provide enough information to instill reasonable doubt in the minds of the jurors, or the information could appear as a shot in the dark. As long as the truth remained in Ishmael's pocket, the rest of the information would just be manipulated by both the prosecution and the defense in order to appear to be true.

- **geisha**   a Japanese girl trained to provide entertaining and lighthearted company, especially for men.

- **cannery**   a processing station for fish.

- **naginata**   a halberd; a weapon consisting of a battle axe and pike, mounted on a handle about six feet long.

- **bugeisha**   a person in military uniform.

- **seppukka**   to take one's own life by using a special and lavishly decorated sword.

- **landlubber** a term used to characterize a person who is clumsy when learning to sail.

- **sea yarn** a tall tale about sailors and sailing.

CHAPTERS 27 AND 28

Finally, Kabuo speaks in his own defense in Chapters 27 and 28. Employing the same technique he used with other characters, Guterson uses flashback to develop Kabuo's character and to narrate events from his point of view.

Kabuo remembers lying to Sheriff Moran during the murder investigation and also remembers lying to Nels Gudmundsson. Nels convinces Kabuo to tell the truth before Kabuo is given the sheriff's report to read; that way, if all the details are consistent, Nels will be able to believe Kabuo. When enticing Kabuo to talk, Nels acknowledges the fact that it is probably difficult to trust the government that treated the Japanese so terribly, but without the truth, Nels wouldn't be able to defend Kabuo, and then Kabuo might be hanged.

Kabuo remembered the foggy night in question, how he almost didn't fish near the shipping lanes for fear of being disoriented and risking an accident. He was having a successful evening when he heard first an air horn and then a familiar voice state, "I'm over here. . . . I'm dead in the water, drifting." The fisherman was Carl Heine.

With dead batteries because of a loose alternator connection, Carl could do nothing but wait and see where he drifted. Kabuo was the first man to come along, and he offered Carl the use of one of his own batteries. Because Carl used a different size battery than Kabuo, Carl used Kabuo's gaff to hammer the flange that was in the battery well and prevented the new battery from fitting. Carl bloodied his own hand while using the gaff.

Kabuo was set to leave when Carl stopped him to talk about the land. Without really negotiating or talking, Carl agreed to sell Kabuo seven acres for the same price Carl himself was paying Ole Jurgensen. They shook on the deal, and Kabuo agreed to put eight hundred dollars down.

Guterson weaves Kabuo's memories seamlessly into the courtroom narrative by ending the memory at the end of Chapter 27 and starting the next chapter with Kabuo on the witness stand. Under cross-examination, Kabuo sticks to his story, even after Alvin Hooks points out that the sheriff's report states that two batteries were found on the *Islander*. Kabuo claims that he simply forgot to mention that he took one from home and installed it before the sheriff arrived. Alvin Hooks maintains that this testimony was just another part of a convenient story that wasn't told three months ago because it didn't exist. As Alvin Hooks finishes his cross-examination, and as Kabuo, the final witness is dismissed, the snowfall finally starts slowing down.

Through Kabuo's experiences and opinions, Guterson confronts racism both directly and indirectly. The exchanges between Kabuo and Nels in the prison cell, as well as the conversation between Kabuo and Carl, verbalize what is often present but not spoken of—feelings of rage, mistrust, and generalizations. Carl apologizes for what has happened, and he and Kabuo come to an understanding. Unfortunately for Kabuo, he can't convince many people of this. His waiting three months, combined with his composure and mannerisms on the stand, causes the courtroom spectators to conclude that he wasn't like them at all. These differences, to them, were not a good thing and almost proof of his guilt.

The prevailing question at the end of Chapter 28 is, "Will the U.S. judicial system prevail without Ishmael's evidence?" Perhaps the differences between Japanese-Americans and Caucasian Americans are too great. Perhaps men are not truly innocent until proven guilty.

- **net drum**   a hollow, revolving cylinder that stores the nets when not in use.

- **reel drive**   the device that uncoils fishing nets.

- **ebb**   the flowing back of tidewater to the ocean.

- **kelp island**   a large mass of brown seaweed.

- **tide drift**   the movement of an unanchored boat as a result of the movement of the ocean tide.

- **whitecaps**   foamy crests at the tops of waves.

- **chop**   a stretch of choppy sea, usually with small waves.

- **surf scoters** sea ducks.

- **murres** narrow-billed, black and white, short-necked diving sea birds.

- **shipping lane** the ocean route prescribed for ships.

- **diaphone** a fog signal that produces a blast of two tones.

- **net gurry** the unusable parts of a sea catch.

- **scupper holes** the openings through the raised upper deck of a ship that allow water to flow overboard.

- **dogfish** sharks, noted for their razor-sharp teeth, that live in the same waterways as the salmon; catching them can cause damage to nets.

- **hake** fish similar to cod.

- **chums** a type of salmon that is undesirable to fishermen because of its bitter taste.

- **black mouth** also called king salmon, desirable deep feeder fish best caught by trolling.

- **binnacle** a case that holds a boat's compass.

CHAPTERS 29 AND 30

The trial ends in Chapter 29, with both lawyers presenting their closing arguments without interruption by Ishmael Chambers. The judge instructs the jury, carefully explaining the charge of murder in the first degree. In Chapter 30, we hear from members of the jury as they deliberate.

In his closing argument, Alvin Hooks presents a scenario that is indeed consistent with the facts, but is of course, incorrect; however, his presentation is not only plausible but also extremely believable. His version makes sense. Then Nels Gudmundsson presents Kabuo's side, taking the narrative a step further. Nels comments upon human nature and prejudice; he wants the jurors to look beyond race, to put the intense feelings of World War II behind them.

Nels provides the moral code of the book as he urges the jurors to look at the facts logically and not emotionally. As he is delivering his closing argument, he is also presenting Guterson's views on racism, prejudice, and the lingering effects they have on not just the island of San Piedro but on the country as a whole. The ideas that Nels leaves with the jury are the ideas Guterson wants to leave with readers—his call to action for all people to examine their own lives and their own actions and do the right thing, the reasonable thing, the one thing that will result in justice—treating one another fairly and objectively.

The jury deliberations provide a means of rehashing and reviewing the testimony. The members of the jury are embattled—eleven versus one. As they attempt to re-create the past, they weigh the evidence, trying to come to the truth, yet only one person is really willing to contemplate "reasonable doubt." Alexander Van Ness recognizes that Kabuo was a liar who may be guilty of something, but he's not convinced that Kabuo is a murderer.

Kabuo certainly did have a jury of his peers, if his peers are represented by all of the inhabitants of San Piedro: Eleven out of twelve islanders do not trust the Japanese, just as eleven out of twelve jurors do not trust Kabuo Miyamoto. At six o'clock, the jury retired for the evening, as torn and divided as Ishmael Chambers.

• **footman**   a male servant.

CHAPTER 31

Ishmael returns to his mother's house, telling her that the jury hadn't reached a verdict. As she clamors that the jury shouldn't be driven by hatred and prejudice, Ishmael ponders his life and his decision. He remembers his father and his father's ways. He recalls working with his father, and re-reads Hatsue's letter.

In doing so, Ishmael comes to understand who he is and his place in the world. He realizes what he has lost was the man he used to be, a man Hatsue admired. He also realizes that his mother is all he has and that he does indeed love his mother. He is struck by the knowledge that when she dies, he will be alone in the world, and ultimately, he decides to take the notes to Hatsue. This action is the climax of the novel.

Providing Hatsue with the notes is the defining moment of Ishmael's life. He had been harboring hate and rage and then nothingness for so long that he prevented himself from living. But just as Hatsue learned from her mother, Ishmael learned from his. His mother never gave up on loving him; he had given up on her and himself. Ishmael's decision signifies significant growth as a person—as a son, a former lover, and a newspaperman. In the search for truth, honor, and justice, Ishmael knew that he had to give the notes to Hatsue.

- **manifest destiny** a future event accepted as inevitable; in the mid-nineteenth century, expansion to the Pacific was regarded as the Manifest Destiny of the United States.
- **Horatio Alger** (1832–1899) American writer of boys' stories.

CHAPTER 32

The final chapter, the resolution, completes the narrative. As Ishmael leaves Hatsue, she gives him the same advice that his mother gave him—to get married and to have children. Hatsue even tells him to live. The next morning, when Hatsue visits Ishmael at his mother's house, he refers to her for the first time as "Mrs. Miyamoto," signifying Ishmael's growth and a change in their relationship.

Using the notes, the sheriff's report, and bits of testimony, Ishmael, joined by Sheriff Moran and Deputy Martinson, investigates the *Susan Marie,* which has been docked at Sommensen's warehouse for the past two and a half months, and pieces together the events of the night. Later that morning, the jury is dismissed, and Kabuo is set free. And Ishmael Chambers ponders the events as he prepares his newspaper article, coming to an understanding "that accident ruled every corner of the universe except the chambers of the human heart." It is no accident that Ishmael turns in the notes he found, for it is the one way that he can provide some semblance of justice in his war-torn world while simultaneously proving his love for Hatsue.

- **creosoted timbers** wood that has been treated with a brownish oily liquid in order to preserve the wood.
- **navigator** a person who steers a course.

- **hard-waked**   the track left by a ship as it moves through the water; as the freighter passed, the water formed waves that struck Carl's boat.

- **dogwatch**   the last night shift.

CRITICAL ESSAYS

NARRATIVE TECHNIQUES: GUTERSON'S LITERARY FORM

Rather than tell a tale by starting at the beginning and following the events in chronological order, Guterson employs a narrative style reminiscent of William Faulkner and Toni Morrison. *Snow Falling on Cedars* combines three basic elements of a circular narrative—the use of the framing technique, the use of flashback, and the use of a limited point of view—to reveal events little by little.

The main story line is the trial of Kabuo Miyamoto. This event itself lasts only three days; however, important information, which is pertinent to the trial, occurred years, even decades, earlier. If a picture frame represented Kabuo's trial, the frame would be comprised of all the events in and out of the courtroom that take place in the present. This frame represents the basic narrative line, yet other stories are told within that main story. These stories, told within the context of the main story, fit within the main frame and serve as a small part of the larger picture. And some of these smaller stories of earlier events frame even smaller stories of even earlier events. Each story is distinct within itself while simultaneously being an integral part of a greater whole; every individual picture is a part of a bigger picture.

This framework technique provides the structure of the plot, and flashback is the technique Guterson uses to tell the stories. Characters reveal these "framed" stories through public testimony on the witness stand and/or private memories. Oftentimes, as in the case with Etta Heine, the reader is privy to a flashback memory that isn't shared with other characters.

The narrator also provides information. The narrator of *Snow Falling on Cedars* provides a limited third-person point of view. This perspective sometimes allows readers into the mind of a character but sometimes does not. This technique is important because it helps to build suspense and intrigue. In addition, this technique allows the story line to flow seamlessly from past to present and back again. A flashback often simultaneously serves as testimony.

Stylistically, the narrative techniques work well because *Snow Falling on Cedars* isn't solely a murder mystery; the book also explores the mystery of relationships and the way people interact with one another. The intricacies of a trial mirror the intricacies of a relationship. Because Guterson's narrative techniques weave two main story lines together, leading to a shared climax, *Snow Falling on Cedars* is a compelling read.

GUTERSON'S USE OF DETAILS

Throughout *Snow Falling on Cedars*, as he tells the story, Guterson scatters seemingly throwaway lines throughout the text. For example, in Chapter 1, he writes, "The accused man, Kabuo, was someone he [Ishmael] knew," not providing any sense of their history. In Chapter 2, Art Moran testifies that "a tin coffee cup lay tipped on its side," though the cup is not mentioned again until 30 chapters later. These lines are important bits of information, or clues, about things to come; this literary technique, known as foreshadowing, is a subtle means of preparing readers for the direction of the narrative. Foreshadowing typically creates suspense and piques the curiosity of the reader. In *Snow Falling on Cedars*, foreshadowing occurs in memories, testimony, and flashbacks.

But not every bit of information foreshadows events (either past or future); some pieces of information exist to provide exquisite imagery and descriptions of people and places. Every word serves a purpose—either advancing the plot or appealing to the senses—so every word is meticulously chosen in order to create a mood, tone, or image. Guterson's use of language is one of the major strengths of his text.

Readers recognizing the importance of small details don't receive only an added appreciation and understanding of Guterson's novel; they also realize a notion that parallels the American judicial system. A need exists for all information, or evidence, no matter how large or small, to be disclosed when trying to establish the guilt or innocence of an accused individual. The specific details often determine the outcome of both a trial and a narrative.

Small details also play an important part in relationships. Just as a mystery depends on clues in order to be solved, a trial depends on evidence in order for a jury to make a decision. Likewise, the success (or failure) of a relationship depends on both the actions and/or inaction of one or both people in that relationship. The bits of information (things that are done or not done) add up to something, the significance of which isn't usually known until time has passed. When a narrative is being told from various points of view and from various time perspectives, it's no wonder that perceptions change throughout the telling. As the evidence unfolds, all the seemingly irrelevant and minor bits of information weave together, forming a telling tapestry, and the "truth" may be greatly different from any of the individual parts.

Although foreshadowing is a literary term, using little bits of information to make larger judgments applies to all aspects of life. That is why recognizing the seemingly trivial or unimportant things plays such an important part in *Snow Falling on Cedars* and plays an important part in one of the themes of the novel. In Chapter 32, Ishmael refers to Hatsue as "Mrs. Miyamoto" for the first time, revealing his growth as a character. This little bit of information, although easily missed, is extremely telling, about both the nature of Ishmael as a character and Guterson as a novelist.

Guterson's incredible attention to detail also helps to give readers a sense of time in the story. The trial lasts only three days, but the memories and the situations leading up to the trial were decades in the making. Lengthy descriptions of the snow outside the courtroom give readers a better sense of what it must be like to be "exiled in the county jail for seventy-seven days" with "no window anywhere in his basement cell, no portal through which . . . light could come to him."

The lengthy description of the forest in which Hatsue and Ishmael meet allows the reader to share in their secret. Guterson acquaints readers with the forest and the hollow in the cedar tree, so that they know it as intimately as the novel's characters. The expansive description of the strawberry fields give a sense of childhood as a length of time. Finally, the amount of detail that Guterson supplies helps the reader understand on an emotional level how slowly time has passed for Ishmael since receiving Hatsue's breakup letter.

DEPERSONALIZATION AND HATE

The connection between the various interrelated themes of injustice, fairness, responsibility, and racism throughout *Snow Falling on Cedars* most often stems from the manner in which characters treat one another. More often than not, various individuals and groups of individuals are depersonalized—treated as less than human—because it's easier to hold on to hate if the hate isn't directed toward a specific person. This depersonalization leads to an effective loss of identity and provides a means for the racist to defer responsibility.

First and foremost, all Japanese people of San Piedro—whether they were citizens or not—were viewed as a group by Carl Heine, Jr., his mother, most islanders, and the United States government. Originally viewed as just berry farmer immigrants, these non-Caucasians were beginning to become problematic, especially during the war. At least, that is what most of the other islanders believed. Curiously, the claim that "we are at war with them" applied only to the inhabitants who looked different than the Caucasians. The most outspoken racist, Etta Heine, was German-born, but nobody cared about that, even though the United States was also at war with Germany. The non-Caucasians were neither people nor neighbors—they were Japs.

Yet, Caucasians weren't the only ones to view the Japanese this way. Neither of Hatsue's parents viewed Hatsue as a woman; instead they saw her as a Japanese woman who happened to be living in America. Just as many of the islanders didn't consider Japanese-Americans to be Americans, Hisao and Fujiko didn't consider themselves or their daughters Americans. The Imadas, although they recognized differences among the Japanese-Americans and the Caucasian Americans and felt superior to them, didn't discriminate. That is an essential difference, which must be noted. Potentially racist thoughts do not necessarily lead to racist actions. Guterson doesn't present all Americans as horrible and all Japanese as wonderful; he presents well-rounded characters who have strong points along with their shortcomings.

This discrimination continued, perhaps even more so after the war, because then the islanders no longer had their convenient excuse that "there's a war going on" to rationalize their behavior. The post-war behavior consisted of treating all Japanese-Americans, regardless of their individual efforts, as less than citizens. As Kabuo sits in that courtroom, he knows that he isn't being viewed as a veteran who sacrificed for his fellow islanders; instead, he is viewed as an outsider, as a Japanese man. Kabuo expresses this sentiment to his lawyer, "'We're sly and treacherous. . . . You can't trust a Jap, can you? This island's full of strong feelings, Mr. Gudmundsson, people who don't often speak their minds but hate on the inside all the same.'"

During the trial, the truth is hidden from the jurors and the spectators, just as all truth is hidden from those who discriminate. Nels Gudmundsson addresses this theme in his closing argument, claiming that people hate because "we are the victims of irrational fears." Depersonalization leads to hate and racism and therefore needs to be eliminated. Nels implores the jurors to consider prejudice and reminds them that "you have only yourselves to rely on." In the same manner, Guterson challenges his readers to brush aside any prejudicial tendencies when seeking out justice, for preserving the dignity and integrity of the individual enables people to eliminate the hate.

PLOT

Two parallel story lines being told throughout *Snow Falling on Cedars* illustrate the importance of point of view. Many times facts end up being distorted, skewed, or conveniently forgotten. In order to have a satisfactory resolution, the two story lines—Kabuo's trial for murder and Ishmael's lost love affair—require insight previously unavailable. This newfound information dramatically changes perceptions and understanding.

In Kabuo's story line, when the truth finally comes to light, obviously the prosecution's entire case is based on an incorrect interpretation of the facts. Circumstantial evidence, mixed with hatred, anger, resentment, and lying, provides jurors with more than enough information to find Kabuo guilty. Ironically, Kabuo does consider himself guilty, but not of the crime with which he is charged. Kabuo's sense of justice goes beyond the courtroom of San Piedro. In fact, it goes beyond the life that Kabuo is currently living. However, his philosophical beliefs and wartime "crimes" have no bearing on the procedures on hand. By the time Hatsue and Kabuo tell the truth about what happened the night of Carl's death, very few are willing to believe him. It doesn't look good for him; however, that is the time Ishmael makes his life-defining decision: He reveals what he knows.

Ishmael makes the decision to do what is ethically and morally right when he finally has an epiphany about the truth regarding his own relationship with Hatsue. For years he has been harboring hate for how she treated him, wallowing in self-pity and unwilling to move on with his life. Ishmael believed for the longest time that he was treated unfairly and was one of the biggest losers because of World War II. This narrow-minded, self-centered approach left him alone in the world. Only re-reading Hatsue's letter from Manzanar and contemplating his life and her views, and his love for her, enabled Ishmael to let go—finally—of all his hurt and pain. Hatsue loved Ishmael enough to be honest with him, and that honesty hurt him. Ishmael happily led the dual life—strangers at school, sweethearts on the weekends—while foolishly thinking that Hatsue felt the same way. After all these years of holding on, Ishmael is finally able to let go. In doing so, he frees both Kabuo and himself.

Had Ishmael not come to an understanding about the nature of his relationship with Hatsue, and had he not revealed the truth about the lighthouse logs, an innocent man would have undoubtedly been found guilty, and an innocent woman would have been beholden to a man who only claimed to love her. The murder mystery and the love story both climax with the appearance of the truth. Only when the truth is known can love survive and justice be served.

CHARACTERS, SYMBOLS, MOTIFS, AND THEMES

Snow Falling on Cedars explores the notions of love and loss as they relate to racism, responsibility, and injustice. Every character in the novel is both directly and indirectly affected by what happens during World War II. For the most part, characters neither take nor accept responsibility for their thoughts and actions, and thus the war becomes the scapegoat.

CHARACTERS

Ishmael and Kabuo. An interesting parallel exists between Ishmael, the protagonist, and Kabuo, the character who would be the main character if *Snow Falling on Cedars* were only a murder mystery. Both island veterans returned scarred from the war but are not considered heroes. Both love Hatsue in the manner in which their respective cultures understand love. And both spend their time after the war carrying a grudge, longing to regain what was lost during the war. Ishmael lost the love of his life, his faith in God, and his arm. Kabuo lost his sense of honor and his family's land. Neither character is happy. In fact, Ishmael's mother is quick to tell him "'That you are unhappy, I have to say, is the most obvious thing in the world.'"

The biggest difference between the two is that Ishmael, in great part due to his anguish over Hatsue, blames the Japanese for his heartbreak and the loss of his arm. When Hatsue sees him after the war and notices his arm, Ishmael angrily says, "'The Japs did it. . . . They shot my arm off. *Japs.*'" Through much of the story, Ishmael is willing to hold an entire race of people responsible for the current state of his life.

Kabuo, on the other hand, feels a huge remorse over and responsibility for his wartime experiences. When Nels Gudmundsson tells him that the prosecution is seeking the death penalty, Guterson explains a key fact about Kabuo: "He was a Buddhist and believed in the laws of karma, so it made sense to him that he might pay for his war murders: everything comes back to you, nothing is accidental."

The last sentence in the novel contrasts Kabuo's religious beliefs with Ishmael's understanding of the world when the reporter comes to understand "that accident ruled every corner of the universe except the chambers of the human heart." When contrasting these two statements, it becomes clear that in spite of their similarities and in spite of their love for Hatsue, these men are very different in their understanding of love, life, and order. And, in many ways, this difference epitomizes the tension between the Japanese and Caucasian islanders.

Hatsue. Hatsue is forced to define herself in terms of either her Japanese or American culture but cannot have both. In order to do this, she lies to the two men in her life whom she loves, yet she lies to them for what she believes are the right reasons. Paradoxically, she comes to an understanding that in every loss there is a gain and in every gain there is a loss.

More than any other character in the book, Hatsue is able to live in the present. When Kabuo comes into her life, she recognizes that she can continue to mourn an impossible romance or create an acceptable life for herself, and so pursues a relationship with a man of her own ethnic heritage in spite of great sadness. From that time forward, she works successfully at putting Ishmael out of her mind. When Ishmael's memory creeps in, "it was not difficult for her, on her wedding night, to then cast Ishmael out of her mind completely; he had only crept in by accident, as it were, because all romantic moments are associated willy-nilly—even when some are long dead."

Both her mother and Mrs. Shigemura emphasize that Japanese women accept life as it befalls them without dwelling on the past, as Guterson explains, "Her [Hatsue's] life had always been strenuous—field work, internment, more field work on top of housework—but during this period under Mrs. Shigemura's tutelage she had learned to compose herself in the face of it. It was a matter in part of posture and breathing, but even more so of *soul*." Later, Hatsue's mother stresses, "The trick was to live here without hating yourself because all around you was hatred. The trick was to refuse to allow your pain to prevent you from living honorably."

Islanders. Most of the islanders continue the wartime prejudices and grudges. Life on San Piedro remains at war. Both sides distrust one another; both sides use wartime events as a basis for the distrust; and both sides really have no desire to find a happy medium. Although the war has ended, battles are still being fought, no doubt because the problems existed before the war began.

Prejudice reared its head in San Piedro when the first Japanese immigrants arrived around 1883. Even then "the census taker neglected to list them by name, referring instead to Jap Number 1,

Jap Number 2, Jap Number 3, Japan Charlie, Old Jap Sam, Laughing Jap, Dwarf Jap, Chippy, Boots, and Stumpy—names of this sort instead of real names."

During the strawberry season, Caucasian and Japanese children work side by side, but otherwise the two cultures keep themselves separate from the other. Children of each group attend school together, but don't acknowledge each other in the hallways. Parents on both sides of the cultural gap warn their children about socializing with the other. Fujiko tells her daughters, "'You must live in this world, of course you must, and this world is the world of the *hakujin* . . . But don't allow living *among* the *hakujin* to become living *intertwined* with them.'" Similarly, when Carl Heine comes home with a fishing rod that Kabuo lent him, Etta insisted that he "take the fishing rod back to the Japs, they owed them money, the rod confused that. . . . 'You turn around and take it right on back.'"

The annual Strawberry Festival is the one time that the two sides come together as one community. The whole town comes in a sort of unspoken truce and "the Volunteer Fire Department played a softball game against the Japanese Community Center Team." Even in their games they are on separate teams. Every year, a young Japanese girl is crowned Strawberry Princess and becomes "an unwitting intermediary between two communities, a human sacrifice who allowed the festivities to go forward with no uttered ill will."

The White islanders divide themselves into two camps regarding interaction with the Japanese. Importantly, Carl Sr. and his wife, Etta, illustrate that two people in the same family can be on opposite sides of the cultural fence. Carl Heine, Sr. was willing to work around the law with Zenhichi as Etta testifies "The Miyamotos . . . couldn't really own land anyway. They were from Japan, both of them *born* there, and there was this law on the books prevented them." Yet as willing as Carl is to work with the Miyamotos, Etta's response is "'We're not such paupers as to sell to Japs, are we?'"

On the fringe of the islanders who have definite opinions are those like Ilse Severensen, people who claim to be fond of the Japanese and treat them well but whose "kindness had always been condescending, and [who] had always paid a bit extra for her berries with the air of doling out charity."

Carl Heine, Jr. Through the trial and the testimony of various witnesses, readers learn a great deal about Carl Heine, Jr. During his adolescence, his mother thinks of him as "a Great Dane puppy, bounding into her kitchen." As an adult, "He was silent, yes, and grave like his mother."

Readers learn the most about Carl from his wife, Susan Marie, but even to her he remains an enigma. Carl was very private, and Susan Marie had a difficult time reading him—"He did not like to explain or elaborate, and there was a part of him she couldn't get to. She attributed this to his war experiences." When Kabuo comes to talk with Carl about the seven acres, Susan Marie can't tell how Carl feels about the Japanese man, his former friend.

Although Carl doesn't appear to carry his mother's prejudices, he does respect her. When talking with his wife about selling the seven acres to Kabuo, Susan Marie expresses concern over how Etta would feel about that. Carl's response is "'It doesn't really come down to her. . . . It comes down to the fact that Kabuo's a *Jap*. And I don't hate Japs, but I don't like 'em neither. It's hard to explain. But he's a Jap.'" With this statement, readers realize that Carl Jr. is a composite of his parents, just as Etta had always hoped he would be.

Throughout the story, various characters explain Carl's quiet nature away as a result of the war. A quiet nature is seen as the sign of "the *good* man." Importantly, Guterson remarks that "San Piedro men learned to be silent." In this place, silence is valued—a trait that the White islanders share with the Japanese.

The fact that Carl is already dead when the story begins is a master stroke on Guterson's part. Readers are left to compose an image of the dead man based on other people's opinions of him and recollections of conversations. At all times, Carl appears to be a guarded man, so any conversations that people report is open to their own interpretation of what he was actually thinking. And because he is dead, readers are never allowed to hear Carl's thoughts as they hear Ishmael's, Hatsue's, and several others'. By the end of the novel, readers know no more about Carl than the characters in the novel do. What would Carl have to say about life on the island? Did Carl really agree to sell Kabuo the seven acres? Did Carl actually believe that Kabuo was a threat to his mother? While characters throughout the story are busy drawing clear lines around black and white, Carl, through death, will always remain a shade of gray. Ultimately, the novel itself doesn't attempt to define right or wrong either. Guterson stays in the gray, leaving the reader to guess what happens next, to define right and wrong, and to discern the meaning of and motivation behind the actions of the novel's central characters.

SYMBOLS

The War and the Trial. Both are life-defining events that unfortunately foster racism and division as well as symbolize justice and injustice. Both events take complicated issues and attempt to present themselves as simplistic either/or options: us versus them, and right versus wrong. Ironically, the government, which was so unjust to Kabuo and basically caused his family's problems, and understandably might not be trusted, is also the institution, right down to his court-appointed lawyer, that Kabuo must trust in order to be cleared of the charges against him.

During both the war and the trial, some townspeople take a stand against racism and injustice. Carl Heine, Sr. is distraught to read that the Japanese have to vacate and have been given only eight days to do so. When Zenhichi comes offering to make a payment on the land, Carl is incredulous, "'Absolutely not,' he said. 'Absolutely not, Zenhichi. We'll get your harvest in, see what comes of that July. Maybe then we can work out something.'" In spite of Etta's protests, Carl has every intention of honoring his business deal with the Miyamotos and fully intends to settle the bill *after* the family returns from their internment.

Ishmael's father, Arthur Chambers, also takes a stand against the injustice that the island's Japanese are facing. He uses his newspaper to show the Japanese in a positive light, telling Ishmael, "'Not every fact is just a fact. . . . It's all a kind of . . . balancing act. A juggling of pins, all kinds of pins." When Ishmael accuses his father of losing his journalistic integrity, Arthur counters with "'But which facts? . . . Which facts do we print Ishmael?'" Ironically, Ishmael must answer the same question when he discovers information that can clear Kabuo. Arthur teaches Ishmael a great lesson when he continues a loosely concealed pro-Japanese stance at considerable cost to his newspaper. Ishmael does not confront that lesson head on, though, until the trial.

During the trial, Nels Gudmundsson shows Kabuo early on that he bears no prejudice, even though he is not Kabuo's lawyer by choice. Nels arrives at Kabuo's cell armed with a chess board and symbolically shows his disinterest in race over a friendly argument about which color chess pieces to play. "'You don't prefer it?' asked Kabuo. 'You prefer white? Or black?'" Nels solves the problem by asking Kabuo to hold one of each color in his hands, choosing "'Left. . . . If we're going to leave it to chance, left is as good as right. They're both the same this way.'"

Those people who don't feel prejudice toward the Japanese hold themselves to a higher moral code than many of the other islanders. Etta remarks on Carl Sr.'s high character without realizing she's doing so: "Stood around evenings up at the pickers' cabins jawing with the Japs and taking pains with the Indians, watching the women weave sweaters and such, drawing the men out on the subject of the old days before the strawberry farms went in. Carl!" Nels alludes to his driving force when he tells Kabuo, "'There are laws. . . . They apply equally to everyone. You're entitled to a fair trial.'"

Snow. Contradictory in nature and interpretation, snow is simultaneously pure and untainted as well as cold and uncaring. It beautifies as it destroys; it covers as it cleanses. Like many of the issues and characters in the novel, complete understanding depends on the point of view from which it is perceived. This dualistic component represents the complexities of all relationships and situations.

Each individual's reaction to the snow is an insight into his or her character. Kabuo sees the snow as "infinitely beautiful" even though it's described as "furious" and "wind-whipped." Kabuo's perception is analogous to the calm exterior he shows in the courtroom and the internal fury he still harbors about his family's land and his wartime experiences. In contrast, Ishmael "hoped it would snow recklessly and bring to the island the impossible winter purity, so rare and precious, he remembered fondly from his youth." Ishmael spends much of the story hoping to recapture the freedom and certainty he felt as a teenager. Hatsue remains in the middle during the snowstorm. To her it is neither beautiful, as Ishmael suggests, nor dangerous—it simply is. Ironically, though, it is Hatsue who looks at the snow and comments, "'Everything looks so pure. . . . It's so beautiful today'" when Ishmael decides to do the ethically correct thing with the information he has about Carl's death.

The fact that the snow falls on cedar trees is important because the hollow of an old cedar tree was the site of Hatsue and Ishmael's secret trysts. As Ishmael comes to terms with his place in life and, more importantly, his place in Hatsue's life, the snow is busily concealing the entrance to the hideout they shared.

Seasons. Guterson uses seasons in the novel to show a progression from youth to maturity, from a certain innocence or naïveté to an awakening of life's realities. Just before finding Carl's body, Sheriff Art Moran sees children playing and thinks *"They're innocent."* At its core, this story deals with lost innocence and the attempts that various characters make to either reclaim it or understand its loss.

Most of the characters' childhood recollections have to do with summer. Ishmael and Hatsue share their first kiss while swimming. The children on San Piedro look forward to picking strawberries in the summer. They "delighted in their field toil in part because of the social life it provided, in part because it furnished the illusion that a job had been included in the summer's proceedings."

Illusion is an important word here. Guterson implies that things of summer—symbolically the things of youth—are an illusion that maturity will erase. Fujiko sums up the transition from youth to maturity when she tells her daughters, "To deny that there was this dark side to life would be like pretending that the cold of winter was somehow only a temporary illusion, a way station on the way to the higher 'reality' of long, warm, pleasant summers. But summer, it turned out, was no more real than the snow that melted in wintertime." With this statement, the reader comes to understand that maturity comes at a price.

Not insignificant, then, is the fact that when Hatsue and Kabuo make love for the first time "Outside snow had drifted against the barracks wall." Hatsue is moving from an immature, springtime sexual experience with Ishmael to a mature sexual experience with her husband in winter. Neither age nor circumstance allowed Hatsue and Ishmael to have a mature sexual relationship. When Hatsue makes love to Kabuo, sexual union is planned between them. With Ishmael a spontaneous "Let's get married" precedes an urgent desire to consummate their relationship. As Hatsue leaves their tree for the last time, she realizes "that they had been too young, that they had not seen clearly, that they had allowed the forest and the beach to sweep them up, that all of it had been delusion," and she is on her way to a mature understanding of intimate love.

Summer is a time of beauty and possibility. Hatsue was "crowned princess of the Strawberry Festival in 1941," a testament to her youthful beauty. Shortly after that, Mrs. Shigemura tells Hatsue that she "should learn to play her hair lovingly, like a stringed musical instrument." But as Hatsue grows older, she no longer wears her hair loose, preferring to wear it in a knot at her neck as her mother does. The freedom of long, flowing hair gives way to the restrictions of adulthood and the reality of Hatsue's life as her hair becomes increasingly contained.

As an adolescent in the summer of his life, Ishmael believes that "from his point of view, at fourteen years old, their love was entirely unavoidable. It had started on the day they'd clung to his glass box and kissed in the sea, and now it must go on forever. He felt certain of this." No matter how improbable the situation, youth gives Ishmael the conviction that he and Hatsue can overcome the barriers that their culture places on them. Ishmael spends much of his adult life trying to find a way to turn this belief, this desire, into reality. It is winter when he realizes that he must let Hatsue go. When Ishmael shares his information about Carl's death with the authorities, he has reached a new level of maturity. In a poignant moment, he acknowledges this shift when he meets with Hatsue and says, "When you're old and thinking back on things, I hope you'll remember me just a little."

Early in the novel, Kabuo realizes during his trial that "He had missed autumn . . . it had passed already, evaporated," and although Guterson doesn't use a great deal of autumn imagery in *Snow Falling on Cedars,* this statement is important. Kabuo misses autumn because he's in a state of suspension—living in jail, not yet free, not yet convicted. For Guterson, fall is the space between in-nocence and maturity. Everything comes into question in the au-tumn. Hatsue starts dating Kabuo in late summer, which is just about the time that Ishmael is going through basic training. Ishmael loses his arm in a battle on November 19, and in his agony blames it on Hatsue. In Hatsue's letter to Ishmael, she tells him, "Your heart is large and you are gentle and kind, and I know you will do great things in this world," but Ishmael counters that with the recognition that "the war, his arm, the course of things—it had all made his heart much smaller." Significantly, then, Ishmael re-claims his large heart in winter by doing great things for Hatsue and Kabuo.

Ishmael falls prey to burgeoning maturity's greatest danger—cynicism. Emotionally, Ishmael is still in that space between sum-mer and winter when he acknowledges that "His cynicism—a veteran's cynicism—was a thing that disturbed him all the time. It seemed to him after the war that the world was thoroughly altered. It was not even a thing you could explain to anybody, why it was that everything was folly." World War II serves as that autumn space for all the characters in the story. What they do with the lessons learned here is up to them.

Kabuo's arrest occurs in the fall, which is another time of sus-pension for the main characters. Though Hatsue has a great deal of support from family and friends, autumn passes for her "with her life arrested, on hold." While Kabuo sits in a literal cell, the trial brings Hatsue and Ishmael to a new point. Thus, Guterson con-firms that even in adulthood, people continue to reach new levels of maturity. Ishmael spends the autumn months wondering whether he can work his way back into Hatsue's life. But in the winter months of the trial, he comes to a mature decision.

Nels Gudmundsson, a man in the "winter" of his life, shows great levels of maturity. Nels is quietly and respectfully logical in the face of great prejudice and emotion when questioning witnesses. "'In your estimation, as a veteran gill-netter, as president of the San Piedro Gill-Netters Association, it isn't possible that the defendant boarded Carl Heine's boat. . . . The problem of a forced boarding precludes that—makes it impossible?'" Further, he holds each wit-ness—including his own client—accountable for telling the truth. When Kabuo lies out of what he believes to be self-defense, he tells

Nels that telling the truth can be difficult. Characteristically, Nels understands Kabuo's reluctance to trust him, but his response is, "'Just the same . . . There are the things that happened . . . and the things that did not happen. That's what we're talking about.'" The fact that Nels is 79 and a bit feeble is important. By describing Nels' disabilities, Guterson gives readers the sense that Nels has experienced a great deal in his life and that his own maturity is hard-won.

Guterson also points to the cyclical nature of seasons and of emotional growth when Hatsue comments to Kabuo, "'A big snow. Your son's first.'" And so the cycle of innocence to maturity comes full circle and begins again.

Boat Names. One of the main questions that Hatsue and other American children born to Japanese parents struggle with in this story is whether "identity was geography instead of blood—if living in a place was what really mattered." For the Caucasians on the island, the fact that they're White is what matters most. They would answer that identity is blood. By naming his boat the *Susan Marie,* after his wife, Carl Heine, Jr. is making a connection to people, to family, to blood. Japanese-born islanders would agree with Heine and many other Caucasians on the island. They encourage their children to marry within their culture. Under Mrs. Shigemura's tutelage, Hatsue is told "that white men carried in their hearts a secret lust for pure young Japanese girls. . . . Stay away from white men . . . marry a boy of your own kind whose heart is strong and good."

No matter how intent these parents are about instilling in their children that they're "first and foremost Japanese," their children who are American by birth and Japanese by heritage have a hard time with this concept. Although they ultimately stay within the culture of their heritage, they are constantly tempted to join the culture of their birthplace. It is no coincidence, then, that Kabuo, "precisely the boy Mrs. Shigemura had described for [Hatsue] so many years ago," owns a boat named the *Islander*, a name of place. Kabuo and Hatsue look forward to returning to San Piedro after the war. They look forward to returning to their place. Though enmeshed in Japanese culture, these people are still torn between heritage and geography.

MOTIFS

Nature Images. Detailed descriptions of wildlife—plants and animals—that are native to the Northwest permeate the pages of Guterson's text. They not only provide a realistic setting but also enable the reader to enter the world of the characters.

Fishing Jargon. Being a fisherman is more than just an occupation; it is a way of life. And although gill-netting is illegal now, then it provided an identity for so many. In order to understand more fully the men and the lives they lead, it is imperative to live in their world.

Japanese Words and Phrases. In order to capture the Japanese culture, Guterson uses Japanese words and phrases throughout his text. Not all terms are fully or easily translated, though, and that raises this question: Is it possible, no matter how hard you try, to understand completely another culture? And if it is not, then are the gaps between cultures able to be crossed?

THEMES

The ideas of racism, justice, and responsibility and the interplay among the three as they relate to decisions made in the lives of people pervade *Snow Falling on Cedars*. These issues are raised in personal relationships, international relationships, the notion of war, and the court of law. At the end of the novel, even though the trial is over and Ishmael has done the honorable thing, questions still remain. And although certain aspects of the issues are laid to rest, the major themes themselves are not laid to rest and cannot provide a sense of closure. Closure is impossible, because every individual who encounters these difficulties in life is facing a personal trial—a trial whose outcome is in his own control. Taking responsibility for one's own actions is the first step toward bridging the cultural gaps.

ROLE OF GENDER IN THE NOVEL

Gender roles are clearly defined for the characters in *Snow Falling on Cedars*. Men are the caretakers and providers, but women are responsible for maintaining the familial and social structure. Gender roles in the story are often most clearly defined by the relationships that the characters have with their parents and spouses.

Decision/Compliance. Women in both cultures have very little say in the decisions their spouses make concerning their families. Etta doesn't want to sell the land to the Miyamotos primarily because they are Japanese, but also because she believes the land will be worth more later. In exasperation, she tells Carl, "'You're the man of the house, you wear the pants, go ahead and sell our property to a Jap and see what comes of it.'" And he does. And indeed, the land is worth more when she sells to Ole Jurgensen a few years later. Still, even after Carl, Sr.'s death, Etta has to act quickly on her decision to sell the land: "Carl junior was away at the war, and Etta took advantage of this circumstance to sell the farm to Ole Jurgensen." In today's society, readers may find it odd that a mother would be beholden to her son, but in 1940s America, this response was typical.

Like her mother-in-law, Susan Marie Heine doesn't want to live on a strawberry farm. Although "she knew how Carl felt about the old place at Island Center and his passion for growing strawberries . . . she didn't want to leave the house on Mill Run Road." And yet the reader clearly understands that the fact that Susan Marie doesn't want to move has no bearing on Carl's ultimate decision to give earnest money to Ole Jurgensen. And when Susan Marie ponders growing older with Carl, "She didn't even want to think about that or to mull how one day they might have nothing except his silence and his obsession with whatever he was working on—his boat, their house, his gardens." Susan Marie is happy in her marriage and she loves her husband, but she has little say in the paths their lives together take.

Similar relationships exist in the island's Japanese marriages. Kabuo enlisted in the service without consulting Hatsue, and "He remembered the expression on Hatsue's face when he told her he had enlisted." She felt very strongly that he shouldn't enlist, but he insisted, "There was this matter of honor . . . and he had no choice but to accept the duty the war imposed on him. . . . love went deep and meant life itself, but honor could not be turned from." Kabuo's wartime experiences fundamentally changed who he is, and

Hatsue had no say in his decision to go to war—a decision that altered the course of her life as well.

Aftermath of War. No San Piedro man wants to talk about his war experiences. Women on the island are left guessing about how men feel. Women find this reluctance to speak both irritating and intriguing. Susan Marie Heine remembers her attraction to Carl. His was an "island boy's face and at the same time mysterious. He'd been to the war after all." Susan finds this mystery extremely appealing, but later comes to the realization that "their sex life had been at the heart of their marriage. It had permeated everything else between them." After marriage, children, and building a life together, Carl remains an enigma to his own wife.

Hatsue's fear when Kabuo enlists in the service is not the separation but the idea that he may come back a different person. He only tells her that he has no choice. Hatsue holds her family together after their return to San Piedro, but during the trial, she accepts that "her husband . . . was a mystery to her, and had been ever since he'd returned from his days as a soldier . . . she was married to a war veteran and that this was the crucial fact of her marriage; the war had elicited in him a persistent guilt that lay over his soul like a shadow."

Late in the course of the trial, Ishmael visits his mother, Helen. They have a detailed conversation about God and other things philosophical. Finally, reaching out, Ishmael asks his mother what he should do. Her answer, "'I can't tell you what to do Ishmael. I've tried to understand what it's been like for you . . . but I must confess that, no matter how hard I try, I can't really understand you. There are other boys, after all, who went to war and came back home and pushed on with their lives . . . despite whatever was behind them.'" Painful as it is for Helen to admit, her only child has become a complete mystery to her since returning from the war. Readers may wonder whether the war or the end of his romantic relationship with Hatsue changed Ishmael, but the fact remains that on a very deep level, his mother can no longer reach him.

Ultimately, the war changes the relationship between the sexes in the novel. In spite of being somewhat limited in the scope of things they can do, women appear in many ways to be stronger than their male counterparts. The men who served in the war come home broken in some way: Carl Jr. is somber and quiet, Kabuo is angry and in jail, and Ishmael is bitter and cynical. The men's battle experiences wrought a drastic change in their personalities. Ishmael's visible loss—his arm—is an allegory for the emotional stump all the island's war veterans carry with them.

In *Snow Falling on Cedars*, men often leave women behind—although not necessarily by choice. Hisao leaves Fujiko when he is sent to an internment camp ahead of his family; Kabuo leaves Hatsue when he enlists in the service; and, Carl Heine, Sr., Carl Heine, Jr., and Arthur Chambers leave their wives in death. Ironic then, is the fact that Hatsue leaves Ishmael, first by being sent away and then by sending him away with her "Dear John" letter.

Women survive capably without their spouses. Etta Heine is able to live independently, as is Helen Chambers. In fact, "Carl had . . . built a big frame house just west of Amity Harbor, including an apartment for his mother. . . . But—out of pride, word had it—Etta would not move in with him." Hatsue has support from her "sisters, cousins, and aunts who called mornings and asked her to come for lunch" during Kabuo's incarceration and is able to manage the household without Kabuo's presence. During a brief visit, Kabuo reminds Hatsue to check their root cellar. She tells him, "'I've been checking. . . . Everything's fine.'" The only man whose wife has preceded him in death is Nels Gudmundsson, Kabuo's attorney, who is "seventy-nine and trapped inside a decaying body." He does not appear to be faring as well as the women who have lost their men in some way. Nels and his wife "had not gotten along particularly well, but nevertheless he missed her." Nels' "hope of rediscovering that lost part of himself he deeply, achingly missed" stands as another symbol for the islanders who lost a part of themselves in battle. San Piedro's men have seen too much, and Nels' eyes—one blind and useless, the other "preternaturally observant"—provide an allegory for that.

Emotion versus Reason. Throughout the novel, highly emotional circumstances spur male characters to action, while the affected females rely on reason.

In their early moments digging clams together, Ishmael uses the ocean as an analogy for how people are ultimately all the same. Practical at a young age, Hatsue replies, "'Oceans don't mix. . . . They're different temperatures. They have different amounts of salt. . . . They're different from each other.'" When Ishmael presses her to explain further, she simply says, "'They just are. . . . Just because.'" As a young adolescent, Hatsue has a better understanding of the way the world works and hints that she understands the problems that will follow her relationship with Ishmael. Ishmael, on the other hand, believes that he can alter the course of the world. He wants to take action.

When the United States goes to war with Japan, Ishmael's first thought is that after the war he and Hatsue will elope to Seattle, where a mixed marriage is more likely to be accepted. He dramatically professes his love for Hatsue and speaks of his grandiose plans for them. As much as Hatsue would like to wrap herself in the warmth of this emotional outpouring, she still says, "'I'm trying to be realistic about this. It isn't that simple, is what I'm saying. There are all these other things.'"

When his family's land is sold to Ole Jurgensen, Kabuo returns to San Piedro angry. He carries that anger with him for nine years. Not having land to farm makes him feel that he is somehow failing his family, and he tries to compensate for that by working extra hard at being a successful fisherman. His emotions over the lost land and his expectations of himself drive him. Hatsue, though, learns to be satisfied with what she has. Although not the life she had in mind when she and Kabuo married, "this house and this life were what she had, and there was no point in perpetually grasping for something other." Hatsue can be content with the life they have because reason leads her to understanding.

Undoubtedly, the main factor behind Etta's resistance to sell their land to the Miyamotos was the fact that the buyers were Japanese. However, readers see Carl Sr. driven by emotion in his decision, which is evident when he says, "'Sure be nice to have the money, though, wouldn't it?'" Etta is more forward thinking and realizes that the payments will be too small to net them any immediate gain: "'He's going to pay up two bits at a time, and you're going to carry it for pocket change to town. . . . Your seven acres is going to be swallowed up by the dime store in Amity Harbor.'" She also realizes that the land will be worth more in time. So, in spite of her prejudice, readers must admit that she has some sound, reasonable concerns about the land sale.

Late in the story, Ishmael has a conversation about God with his mother. Ishmael doubts God's existence, while Helen explains that belief itself is a leap of faith, a feeling people get that brings a certain understanding. Ishmael responds by saying, "'I don't feel what God is. . . . I don't feel anything either way. No feeling about it comes to me. . . . I can't make a feeling like that up, can I?'" Ishmael fancies himself based in reason during this conversation, but he fails to realize that cynicism is often emotional. His mother is free of cynicism in spite of the hardships she's endured and thus is more open to reasonable possibilities.

Personal Freedom. Women experience personal freedom very differently in the story than men do. Hatsue's parents keep close tabs on her and are strict with her. Though she routinely steals away to meet Ishmael, in a conversation with her mother, "Hatsue knew then that her pretense had failed her. . . . Now her mother seemed to know the truth, or to have some inkling of it." Hatsue exists in a world of constricted freedom. Yet, Ishmael's parents never question where he spends his afternoons or with whom. Helen seems to have no knowledge of any sort of relationship between her son and a Japanese girl, while Fujiko is well aware of the influence the *hakujin* have on her eldest daughter. Would the situation have been different if Hatsue was a Japanese boy and Ishmael a white girl? Would Ishmael's parents have kept a closer watch? Would Hatsue's parents have been so reticent about the relationship? Readers can only guess.

Pretty women have more leeway within a world that doesn't offer them a great deal of personal freedom. When Susan Marie reflects on meeting her husband, she fully recognizes that "She'd met Carl Heine because she'd wanted to meet him. On San Piedro a woman with her looks could do such a thing if she did it with proper innocence." Women in this community are held to certain standards, certain ideals of womanhood. If they meet them, they can move more freely than those who rebel.

Etta Heine and Helen Chambers have a unique way of gaining freedom for themselves after their respective husbands die. Etta sells the strawberry farm she never liked and moves into a one-bedroom apartment in town. She arranges her finances so that she has "enough money to get by on, if she was mindful of her pennies. Fortunately, this mindfulness accorded with her nature." Helen refuses to leave her home during the snowstorm, even though going into town would probably be safer for her. Out of concern, Ishmael goes to stay with Helen, although he recognizes that "His mother, at fifty-six, was the sort of country widow who lives alone quite capably." When he arrives, Helen has already taken care of the chores and has a pot of soup cooking on the stove.

Parenthood. Fathers appear to be less involved in child-rearing than mothers in the story. The most important exchanges between Fujiko and Hatsue occur when Hisao isn't with them. Fujiko effectively ends Hatsue's relationship with Ishmael when she discovers his letter to her daughter. Though Hatsue insists that she had decided not to write back, the reader knows that more likely her resolve would have melted. When Hatsue apologizes for her deception, her mother says, "'Deceiving me . . . is only half of it, daughter. You have deceived yourself, too.'" Importantly, Fujiko speaks these words in Japanese, which is a subtle way of reminding Hatsue that she is a Japanese woman, separate from the *hakujin*.

Etta Heine plays a major role in her son's life as well. Though he has many of his father's ways, the war sways him toward many of Etta's prejudices—prejudices she uses to her advantage. She testifies that Carl "'Said that if Kabuo Miyamoto was giving me dirty looks he'd keep an eye on him.'" Her lessons of exclusion stay with Carl into his adult life. Readers can only wonder what influence she had on her other three children—whose names aren't provided, which is significant given Guterson's level of detail. The three of them left San Piedro. "Only the second—Carl junior—returned."

Ishmael's father teaches his son the journalism business and impresses his son with his nonprejudiced standards. Ishmael learns his craft from his father. But Ishmael's mother, Helen Chambers, teaches him about survival, about bearing great loss. Ishmael visits his mother during the snowstorm and realizes, "His mother had gone cold when Arthur died; her grief for him was fixed. But this had not stopped her from taking pleasure in life." Helen uses Ishmael's close relationship with Arthur to help her son deal with his pain. She reminds him that Arthur served in World War I and that he had a hard time dealing with the aftermath of that war, but "'He went right on with his life. He didn't let

80

self-pity overwhelm him—he just kept on with things.'" While Fujiko teaches her children how to be Japanese in a white world, Helen teaches Ishmael how to live with himself.

Curiously, little mention is made of Kabuo's mother. His important life lessons come from his father, who informs him of his samurai heritage and teaches him *kendo*. Zenhichi teaches Kabuo to keep his anger in check by saying, "'My grandfather was an expert swordsman . . . but his anger overwhelmed him in the end.'" Like Fujiko with Hatsue, Zenhichi speaks in Japanese as he teaches his son. During his trial, Kabuo reflects on the anger he harbored during the war, thinking that "Perhaps it was now his fate to pay for the lives he had taken in anger." Readers are left to ponder what feminine influence Kabuo had in his life and what difference it might have made.

Now mothers themselves, Hatsue Miyamoto and Susan Marie Heine are raising the next generation of island children. Readers are left wondering whether Hatsue will be as insistent as her mother was that her children remain tied to Japanese culture. Will Susan Marie continue to perpetuate the prejudice in her children that Etta Heine did in Carl Jr.?

USE OF DUALITY IN THE NOVEL

Guterson makes extensive use of dualism or dichotomy in *Snow Falling on Cedars*. In literature, this device allows the author to explore the main themes of the novel by comparing two things that contrast each other within the story.

Japanese and White. Probably the most obvious dualism in the story is that of San Piedro's Japanese and White populations. The two populations don't make much effort to understand each other's culture, even though children of both races attend the same schools and pick strawberries together in the summer time.

The Japanese hold no positions of power in the San Piedro community, as evidenced by the fact that "the foreman, a white man" oversees their picking. Guterson's decision to add the "white man" qualifier further suggests the separation and balance of power that exists between the two races. In fact, the only time the groups come together in any meaningful way is for the annual

Strawberry Festival. The day after the strawberry festival "at noon traditionally, the Japanese began picking raspberries." Note that Guterson makes no mention of Whites working in the berry fields after the Strawberry Festival. Certainly, the White islanders went back to work the next day as well, but by omitting that information, Guterson implies that the Japanese are held to a different set of standards than their White peers.

The Japanese certainly hold themselves to a different standard. After the attack on Pearl Harbor, Fujiko gathers her daughters to remind them of their role as Japanese women. She sums up the difference for Hatsue when she says, "'We bend our head, we bow and are silent, because we understand that by ourselves, alone, we are nothing at all, dust in a strong wind, while the *hakujin* believes his aloneness is everything, his separateness is the foundation of his existence. He seeks and grasps . . . for his separateness, while we seek union with the Greater Life—you must see that these are distinct paths we are traveling . . . the *hakujin* and the Japanese.'"

One of the primary differences in the two culture's outlook on life stems from their religions. The Whites on the island are Christian, while the Japanese are Buddhists. These religions are very different in their approach to living, but neither side makes any attempt to understand the other's religion. When Etta Heine looks at Zenhichi Miyamoto, she notices that he hasn't aged the same way that she has and thinks that "something he knew about kept him from aging . . . something he knew about yet kept to himself, . . . Maybe it was Jap religion." Etta shows no interest in learning the first thing about the "Jap religion" but instead holds it against Zenhichi and his religion that the man shows little signs of aging.

Throughout the novel, Guterson portrays the extreme difficulty in this division for those children born in the United States to Japanese parents. This problem follows them into adulthood. When Kabuo is helping Carl Jr. on his boat, Carl begins to talk about "fighting you goddamn Jap sons a—." Kabuo reacts strongly, especially since Carl's mother is German, saying "'I'm an American. . . . Just like you or anybody. Am I calling you a Nazi, you big Nazi bastard? I killed men who looked just like you—pig-fed German bastards. I've got their blood on my soul, Carl, and it doesn't wash off very easily.'"

82

Justice and Injustice. Justice means different things to different characters in *Snow Falling on Cedars,* and Guterson never provides a final answer to the question of what is just or what is unjust.

Etta and Susan Marie Heine want to see Kabuo brought to justice, believing that he murdered Carl junior. Hatsue wants to see justice served by proving Kabuo's innocence. She is committed enough to this quest to ask Ishmael to write about the inaccuracies and prejudices being displayed as evidence in the trial. Ishmael admits that the trial is unfair on many levels but only goes so far as to offer to write an opinion piece about "How we all hope the justice system does its job." Hatsue presses, and Ishmael gives insight to the other side of the justice question: "sometimes I wonder if unfairness isn't . . . part of things. I wonder if we should even expect fairness, if we should assume we have some sort of right to it."

Ishmael's statement initially sounds like more cynicism, but given all that he's experienced, he has a point. Was it just that he and Hatsue spent the entire course of their romantic involvement in the hollow of a cedar tree? Was it fair that the society they lived in wouldn't allow them to spend their lives together—wouldn't even acknowledge that their love could be real? What justice was there in losing his arm or in watching helplessly as his friends were brutally killed in battle?

Because Buddhists believe in the karmic laws that say that everything you do—good or bad—comes back to you, Kabuo believes in some way that he deserves to suffer for a crime he didn't commit. The men he killed on the battlefield weigh heavily on him, so much so that "He felt he did not deserve for a moment the happiness his family brought to him, so that . . . he imagined that he would . . . leave them and go to suffer alone, and his unhappiness would overwhelm his anger. . . . Sitting where he sat now . . . it seemed to him he'd found the suffering place he'd fantasized and desired." This sort of sentiment would not make sense to the White islanders, but for Kabuo, it is in perfect keeping with his religious beliefs.

At the end of the novel, Guterson leaves many questions of justice unanswered. True, Kabuo is proven innocent, but will the islanders accept his innocence or will they always be suspicious of him as a murderer? Kabuo's lifelong dream has been to reclaim what he believes to be his family's land. Carl junior was finally going to make that dream a reality. The land is presumably still for sale, but will Ole sell to Kabuo now? Will Kabuo feel that he has paid the price for his war killings, or is he destined to a lifetime of anguish? At the novel's end, Ishmael is still a weary, one-armed, war veteran. This man will never find justice for losing the love of his life (or his arm), but readers are left without any indication of whether Ishmael finds some happiness. By not answering these and other questions, Guterson, some may say, is unjust to the readers. And therein lies the brilliance. By leaving questions unanswered, Guterson, in a subtle way, helps readers experience the feelings of injustice his characters face.

Innocence and Guilt. Piggybacking the questions of justice and injustice are those of innocence and guilt. In *Snow Falling on Cedars,* innocence and guilt go far beyond whether or not Kabuo Miyamoto murdered Carl Heine, Jr.

Although Etta Heine was within her legal rights when she sold her farm to Ole Jurgensen, she is still guilty of a wrongdoing. Characteristic of someone who is guilty of a moral crime, Etta becomes very defensive, stating on the witness stand that "'Them Japanese couldn't own land. . . . So I don't see how them Miyamotos could think they owned ours.'" Etta's guilty conscience becomes more clear when the judge has to remind her that this trial does not involve real estate. Etta makes a feeble attempt to ease her guilt by sending the Miyamotos their equity in the land after she resells it to Ole Jurgensen.

The relationship between Hatsue and Ishmael can be held up to the magnifying glass of guilt versus innocent as well. During one of many meetings in the cedar tree, Hatsue "confessed to experiencing a moral anguish over meeting him so secretly and deceiving her mother and father. It seemed to her certain that she would suffer from the consequences of it, that no one could maintain such deceit for so long without paying for it somehow." But Ishmael insists that "God could not possibly view their love as something wrong or evil." In this case, guilt or innocence is an internal feeling. Ishmael is deceiving his parents about his relationship with a Japanese girl, just as Hatsue is deceiving hers. Yet, Ishmael feels no remorse, and so deems himself innocent. Hatsue feels perpetual remorse and so condemns her own actions.

Similarly, the war raises the same sorts of questions for Kabuo. He is a consummate soldier, but "It was only after he'd killed four Germans that Kabuo saw . . . He was a warrior, and this dark ferocity had been passed down in the blood of the Miyamoto family and he himself was fated to carry it into the next generation." Because of his religious beliefs, Kabuo believes that now "his suffering inevitably would multiply." Yet, men go to war to kill other men. Kabuo enlisted because he felt honor bound to defend the United States of America. Killing is a sad fact of war, but Kabuo punishes himself for his actions.

Kabuo is guilty of lying to his lawyer: "For when Nels Gudmundsson had asked for his side of the story . . . two and a half months ago he'd stuck with the lie he'd told Sheriff Moran: he didn't know anything about it, he'd insisted, and this had deepened his problems." Kabuo lies because he believes that doing so is in his best interest. After all, who's going to believe a Japanese man who's had a fairly public feud with the murdered man's family? But in trying to protect his innocence, Kabuo only appears more guilty. When the prosecuting attorney questions Kabuo, all he can say is "'For the life of me I can't understand why you didn't tell this story from the start.'" Later in Kabuo's testimony, Alvin Hooks brings up his lies again saying, " 'Mr. Miyamoto . . . You are under oath here to tell the truth. You're under oath to be honest with the court, to be forthcoming with the truth about your role in the death of Carl Heine. And now it seems to me that once again you wish to change your story." Kabuo Miyamoto becomes his own worst enemy.

The real questions of guilt and innocence, though, Guterson leaves for the readers to decide. Does Etta owe anything to the Miyamoto family beyond the equity she paid them? Does Ole Jurgensen owe any consideration to Kabuo? Was Jurgensen wrong to buy the seven acres that he knew the Miyamotos were leasing? Does Carl junior owe anything to Kabuo? Is he morally charged with carrying out his father's wishes? Does the jury have a responsibility beyond the evidence? Is Hatsue guilty for loving Ishmael? Is Fujiko correct in forcing an end to Hatsue's relationship with Ishmael? As a reporter, is Ishmael responsible for commenting on his opinions of the trial? If he can sway public opinion, does he have a responsibility to try to do so?

Fishing and Farming. The two main occupations on San Piedro are salmon fishing and strawberry farming. The differences and similarities between these two professions help readers better understand the motivation of certain characters in *Snow Falling on Cedars*. Farming depends on daylight, but fishing is a nighttime endeavor. Both Carl Jr. and Kabuo want to be farmers but are forced to be fishermen. Yet these former friends are tied together by a bamboo fishing rod. The night Carl needs help on the *Susan Marie*, he says, "'you know what else Kabuo? I still got your bamboo fishing rod. I kept it all these years. I hid it in the barn after my mother tried to make me go and return it over to your house.'" Ironically, fishing is the first evidence readers see of Carl's friendship with Kabuo, and it is what ultimately what brings them back together; but, just as each man is about to realize his dream, the fishing waters steal it from both of them.

The heat and light in the strawberry fields during the summer are intense. During the summers in the fields, Hatsue "wore a straw hat low on her head, a thing she had not done consistently in her youth, so that now around her eyes there were squint lines." But fisherman work in the dark. The night Carl dies, Kabuo hears one fisherman complain to another that the fog is so thick "'I near can't see my own hands. . . . I near can't see the nose on my own face.'" Metaphorically, Carl and Kabuo are moving toward the light—a life of farming, a fulfillment of their dreams. Ironically, Kabuo finds Carl on the water holding a lantern: "And this was how he had found Carl Heine, his batteries dead, adrift at midnight, in need of another man's assistance. There Carl stood in the *Islander*'s spotlight a big man in bib overalls poised in his boat's bow, a kerosene lantern clutched in one hand and an air horn dangling from the other."

Carl and Kabuo are now mutually dependent on each other. The White man needs help from Kabuo getting his boat to run in a soupy fog; the Japanese man needs help from Carl to get his farm back. Moreover, Carl fought the Japanese in World War II—Kabuo fought the Germans. In these dark waters, alone, the men have an opportunity to bury some of the harsh feelings that exist between the Japanese and the White islanders. Ultimately, Kabuo recognizes that "What Carl felt he kept inside, showing nothing to anyone—as Kabuo himself did, for other reasons. They were more similar in their deepest places than Kabuo cared to admit." Perhaps more than any other moment in *Snow Falling on Cedars*, this exchange proves Ishmael's assertion that "'The main thing is, water is water. Names on a map don't mean anything. Do you think if you were out there in a boat and you came to another ocean you'd see a sign or something?'" Not coincidentally then, it is on the water that Kabuo and Carl realize they are more alike than different—right down to their beautiful wives and three young children.

REVIEW QUESTIONS AND ESSAY TOPICS

(1) Kabuo's trial provides a framework for the plot of the novel and becomes an extended metaphor for issues of justice and injustice. Which are the most important judicial issues raised in the text? In *Snow Falling on Cedars*, is justice served both legally and morally?

(2) Discuss the symbolism of snow, particularly during the trial, as well as the role of other types of weather experienced throughout *Snow Falling on Cedars*. How does Guterson use this weather motif to characterize various but interrelated themes found in the text?

(3) *Snow Falling on Cedars* is often characterized as "a novel of place." What are the significant places in the text? What occurs in each? Compare and contrast the mood and tension found in the various settings and the role each provides in both character and plot development.

(4) How does the novel's title characterize and symbolize the major themes of Guterson's text?

(5) Guterson told *People* magazine that, as a writer, "I want to explore philosophical concerns." What are the major philosophical concerns in *Snow Falling on Cedars*? Guterson differentiates between "asking questions" and "providing answers." What questions does he raise in the novel, and why doesn't he answer the questions he asks?

(6) Racism is a central theme of the book. Which characters are most guilty of racist actions? Racist thoughts? Is there a difference? Are the Nisei, American children with Japanese parents, guilty of any form of racism? Are their parents?

(7) Is *Snow Falling on Cedars* primarily a novel about a lost life, lost land, or a lost love? How are the threads of these diverse story lines woven together to provide the truth at Kabuo's trial?

(8) Compare and contrast Guterson's description of the Japanese internment with that presented in *Farewell to Manzanar*, by Jeanne Wakatsuki Houston and James Houston. Focus on the perceptions that the different generations of Japanese-Americans had of the American government. How has this experience subsequently shaped their lives?

(9) *Snow Falling on Cedars* is considered literary fiction. What distinguishes literary fiction from popular fiction? Which elements of literary fiction are best illustrated in the novel? What other contemporary novels are classified as literary fiction?

(10) Compare and contrast the character development of the protagonist in *Snow Falling on Cedars* with that in *The Shipping News*, by E. Annie Proulx. Besides both being newspapermen, what do Ishmael Chambers and Quoyle have in common, particularly because both are the unlikely heroes of their respective tales? Why were both *Snow Falling on Cedars* and *The Shipping News* literary award winners?

(11) Guterson has admitted the influence that Harper Lee's *To Kill a Mockingbird*, his favorite book, has had on his life and his writing. What are the strongest similarities between *Snow Falling on Cedars* and *To Kill a Mockingbird*, and how does Guterson use Lee's text as a springboard for his own storytelling?

(12) Although *Snow Falling on Cedars* is set in 1954, some of the thematic issues play an important role in society today. Do the issues raised in the novel transcend time and place and therefore affect the present, or is the novel depicting a part of history that has no direct bearing on contemporary society?

(13) What is the significance of Ishmael's name? As a character, how is he related to the narrator of *Moby Dick* and the Old Testament brother to Isaac, son of Abraham?

(14) *Snow Falling on Cedars* appears to focus primarily on male characters—Kabuo, Ishmael, Carl—but two women play pivotal roles. Determine the significance Hatsue and Etta have in the events that transpire, particularly how the novel's past pertains to its present time. How do Hatsue and Etta reflect the role that women have in their respective societies?

(15) What is revealed and/or explained in the last line of *Snow Falling on Cedars*: "Accident ruled every corner of the universe except the chambers of the human heart," and why is it significant that Ishmael had this understanding?

(16) Guterson tells several stories in one in *Snow Falling on Cedars:* Hatsue and Ishmael's romance; Kabuo's trial; the effect of World War II on the men who served; the treatment of the Japanese on San Piedro, particularly during World War II; Hatsue's coming to terms with her ethnicity; and the land struggle between the Heines and the Miyamotos. Choose one of these story lines and answer the following questions. If Guterson had told only this story, how would the novel have been different? How would it be the same? Could Guterson tell only one story without bringing in the others? Would the ending be different? Would you perceive any of the characters differently?

(17) If you were a member of the jury, would you have voted Kabuo guilty or not guilty? Why or why not? Remember that as a jury member you have no knowledge of the lighthouse records or of any conversations outside the courtroom.

Concentrating only on the testimony and the questioning, assign and defend your verdict.

(18) Kabuo, a Japanese-American, fought Germans during the war; Carl, a German, fought the Japanese during the war. Why did Guterson choose to have these characters fight against the opposite racial group? If Kabuo and Carl had fought against men who shared their own ethnic backgrounds, how might their relationship have been different? Would Kabuo's guilt be greater if he'd killed other Japanese?

(19) Guterson makes no mention of the atomic bombing of Japan in *Snow Falling on Cedars,* yet in 1954 all the characters would be painfully aware of the way the war ended. Why does Guterson omit that aspect of World War II? How would the story be different if he had included the bombing? How would the characters, especially the island's Japanese and people like Etta Heine, be different?

(20) Compare Nels Gudmundsson with Ishmael Chambers. How are the men alike? How are they different? Although they both reluctantly help Kabuo, are their motivations ultimately the same? Would either man feel differently if Kabuo were a White man? What if Kabuo was White and Carl Japanese? Would Nels act differently if Kabuo hired him? Would Ishmael react differently if Kabuo wasn't Hatsue's husband? As Nels and Ishmael ultimately come to grips with the reality of their lives, how are their responses and choices similar or different?

PROJECTS

(1) Hatsue questions whether identity is a question of geography or blood. The United States has been and continues to be home to many immigrants. Oftentimes, parents in these families tend to cling to the traditions and beliefs of their original country while their American-born children embrace American ideals.

Create a collage that shows in which ways you identify yourself by your ethnic heritage and which ways you identify yourself by where you live. Present the project to your class, explaining whether you believe place or heritage is more important in forming your identity and why.

(2) Hold a town meeting of sorts where Ishmael and Hatsue's romantic relationship is on trial. Choose one character from the novel to portray. When it is your turn to speak, state whether or not the relationship is acceptable. Defend your position as you believe that character would. Be prepared to debate your position.

(3) Guterson's novel is rich in detail about things that are common on Puget Sound. Create a display of things that are unique to the area in which you live. How would these things help outsiders understand you? How do they help you understand yourself? If you were unfamiliar with the items in your display, how might you view these things differently?

(4) Record the images you have of World War II based on movies, books, studies, and conversations you've seen or had. Then collect photos from World War II. Do the photos change your perceptions or strengthen them? What role does propaganda play in the photos and how does that work to mold your impressions? Do the photos change your perception of the role of race in this war? Present your findings to your class.

(5) Assume the role of one of the parents in *Snow Falling on Cedars*. Write letters to three other characters in the story that explain your understanding of life on San Piedro after the war.

(6) Guterson makes extensive use of symbolism throughout *Snow Falling on Cedars*. Draw a picture that uses symbolism to illustrate one of the main themes of the story. Choose from one of the following: forbidden love, racial tension, internment, war, or the struggle of trying to live in two cultures at once.

(7) Imagine that you are Hatsue or Ishmael and that you had married. Today, you are a senior citizen. Looking back over the years, write an article that addresses some of the challenges you've faced as a couple. How well has your marriage survived? How have your children been treated? Were you able to stay in San Piedro? How do you feel about yourself and your decision looking back? What was your relationship with your parents like after your marriage? What have you had to give up to be in this marriage? What have you gained by staying in this marriage? Would you make the same choice again?

(8) Ironically, Etta Heine endures very little prejudice as a German during World War II, while the Japanese suffer considerably. Research the attitude of Americans toward different ethnic groups during the 1930s and 1940s, especially World War II. Write a paper that examines racial relations in the United States across several ethnic groups during this time frame. Discuss how your findings change or confirm your perception of the characters in *Snow Falling on Cedars*.

SELECTED BIBLIOGRAPHY

BOOKS AND ARTICLES

"DAVID GUTERSON." *Contemporary Literary Criticism*. Volume 91. Detroit: Gale Research, 103–108.

"DAVID GUTERSON." *Current Biography*. November 1996. New York: H. W. Wilson, 183–85.

HOCHMAN, DAVID. "Roughing It," *Entertainment Weekly*, April 23, 1999, 28–30.

HOUSTON, JEANNE WAKATSUKI, AND JAMES HOUSTON. *Farewell to Manzanar*. Boston: Houghton Mifflin, 1973.

LEVINE, ELLEN. *A Fence Away from Freedom.* New York: Putnam, 1995.

ONLINE RESOURCES

Centennial High School Book Group. www2.bitstream.net/
~mnyman/snowfall

"Japanese American Exhibit and Access Project."
www.lib.washington.edu/exhibits/harmony

"Japanese American Internment On-Line Exhibit."
www.scuish.scu.edu/SCU/Programs/Diversity/exhibit1

KANNER, ELLEN. "A Wonderful Irony: The Quietest of Books Makes the Splashiest Debut." Interview with David Guterson.
www.bookpage.com/9601bp/fiction/snowfallingoncedars

"Reading Group Guide to *Snow Falling on Cedars.*"
www.randomhouse.com/vintage/read/snow

SHERWIN, ELISABETH. "New Writer Thanks Harper Lee for Leading Way." November 12, 1995. www.dcn.davis.ca.us/
go/gizmo/cedars

NOTES

NOTES

NOTES

NOTES